GREAT MOMENTS IN SPORT:
Show Jumping

Colonel Harry Llewellyn on Foxhunter, the original show
jumping "star"

GREAT MOMENTS IN SPORT:
Show Jumping

DORIAN WILLIAMS

PELHAM BOOKS

First published in Great Britain by Pelham Books Ltd
52 Bedford Square, London, W.C.1
1973

ISBN 0 7207 0680 7

Set and printed in Great Britain by
Tonbridge Printers Ltd, Tonbridge, in Baskerville eleven on
thirteen point on paper supplied by P. F. Bingham Ltd
and bound by Dorstel Press, Harlow

CONTENTS

ILLUSTRATIONS

To the memory of my father
Col. V. D. S. Williams
without whose foresight as a co-founder
of the International Horse Show in 1907
and the British Show Jumping Association
in 1922 there may never have been most of
these great moments

Introduction

The history of show jumping covers three phases. First there are the early days of show jumping which started just about one hundred years ago when it could scarcely be considered a major sport at all. Rather it was a form of cavalry training – called 'show jumping', incidentally, because in contrast to jumping in the hunting field or across country it was jumping in a show ring.

The second phase was between the two World Wars when to all intents and purposes it was a sport that was almost entirely confined to the military. Certainly there were no teams, in any country, other than military teams, cavalry officers more often than not riding horses provided by the army as 'chargers'. Since it was considered a good thing for a regiment to succeed in competitive show jumping for reasons of prestige, so the Army was agreeable to horses of fair calibre being purchased as chargers in the hope that they would become successful show jumpers. Most of them, as often as not, also did their fair share of hunting.

It should not, however, be forgotten that between the wars there were a number of highly successful civilian riders, though, like the Irish riders until a few years ago, when they made an international team it was always in effect a military team.

These early civilian riders, people of the calibre of Tommy Glencross, the Taylor and Foster brothers, the Miss Bullows and others mentioned in an early chapter of this book, made great reputations for themselves and were really the backbone of the early B.S.J.A. The majority of them had professional backgrounds and either rode for others in a professional capacity, or schooled and trained other people's horses, or ran riding schools.

The third phase, of course, starts immediately after the Second World War and stretches right down to the present day. This quarter century sees show jumping really coming into its own, sees it becoming a highly successful and popular sport with the general public – on television it is the second most popular sport now to professional soccer: and sees it attracting a constantly increasing number of actual competitors both young and not so young.

More than these things, it is now a highly organised sport with strict rules and a strongly enforced code of behaviour. Few sports, in fact, are better administered.

Not surprisingly, during these three phases, stretching over a hundred years, there have been many memorable moments, but obviously it is not easy to recall more than a handful of them; those, for the majority, come within living memory.

Yet it would be a mistake either to think that only the third phase – show jumping since the last war – has produced the great moments in show jumping: or that it is only the really great occasions, the Olympic Games, the European Championships, the major international shows, that are capable of producing the great moments.

It must also be true that what is a great moment for one viewer or spectator will be nothing very particular for another. Atmosphere plays a major part, as does the personality of a rider. To some, perhaps, no moment in show jumping can be considered really great unless it involves a Harvey Smith, a Pat Smythe, a Tommy Glencross or even a Lt. Bizard of pre-First World War days. Others will have different heroes and only want to recall *their* exploits.

But if one can remain detached and if one is fortunate, as I have been, to span something like half a century of show jumping – from boy to 'veteran commentator' as I was recently described in a television programme! – then one appreciates, I think, that great moments in any sport can come in all guises.

In one of the following chapters I have recalled the competition which was to make the first major impact on me. Many others who watched it – it was long before the days of television – would probably scarcely give it a thought were they asked to compile great moments.

Obviously there are 'common denominators'. In other words most people would include Col. Harry Llewellyn and Foxhunter clinching the Helsinki Gold Medal: most people would include David Broome and Sunsalve: Pat Smythe would surely find a place with one or other of her triumphs: Harvey Smith and that Hickstead Derby could confidently be expected to appear in any collection of major show jumping occasions.

It is extraordinary how ephemeral a personality in any branch of the entertainment business can be. Speaking to a young audience recently I was astonished to find that the name of Pat Smythe meant almost nothing. It was Ann Moore who was the heroine.

Yet speaking to older generations I find that Pat Smythe and Tosca and Prince Hal mean far more to them than Marion Mould or Ann Moore. Nizefella is still much more of a character than, say, Everest Snaffles; Red Admiral is still remembered while, say, Firecrest is forgotten.

But this, of course, is the case with any sport. For older cricket fans it is Woolley, Gilligan, Hobbs, Bradman, while the English team in India 1972/73 seems to consist of nonentities: but your schoolboys of the seventies know mostly about Illingworth, d'Oliveira, Greig, Underwood. Hammonds, Comptons, Cowdreys, Dexters are scarcely names to them.

It is the same with show jumping. Inevitably after the televising of a show such as the Horse of the Year Show older viewers write to ask what has happened to Vibart or Nugget or Uncle Max or Goodbye – probably implying that the jumpers of today are not the characters that the jumpers of yesterday were: but younger viewers are concerned only with Harvey Smith and Ann Moore, Paddy McMahon and Derek Ricketts: though evergreens such as Alan Oliver, Peter Robeson, Ted Edgar, Ann Backhouse marvellously bridge the generation gap.

In selecting, therefore, a dozen or so great moments from fifty years of show jumping one has to try to take into consideration all the factors referred to above.

On a handful of occasions, such as the Helsinki Olympics, Sunsalve's round in the Rome Olympic Games, Paddy McMahon and Pennwood Forge Mill's triumph at the eleventh hour against the might of Germany at the 1972 Horse of the Year Show, the Harry Llewellyn–Pat Smythe duel at Harringay – on such occasions the atmosphere generated by the performance makes the occasion something unforgettable, something classic.

Others seem to me to justify inclusion in a book such as this – and twenty different writers would include twenty different highlights – for a variety of reasons, personal, sentimental, dramatic, unexpected, satisfying.

In making my choice of great moments, I have tried to cover as wide a field as possible, attempting to show that in jumping it takes all sorts of different occasions, different conditions, different personalities, to create a big moment, admitting always that what is a big moment for one person will not be particularly big for another.

Deliberately I have not arranged the various events in chronological order.

It is probably true to say that certain riders, the d'Inzeos, Hans Winkler, Harvey Smith, David Broome, Pat Smythe, Seamus Hayes have had between them more great moments than all the other riders put together: but deliberately I have not told of endless successes of these household names, for fear of being repetitious.

It seems to me that it is likely that the ordinary reader

will be more interested to read of a fairly wide variety of horses and riders rather than to read constantly of the same people stepping from mountain peak to mountain peak. Just sometimes it is, one dares to suggest, interesting to read of the mighty fallen as well.

Show jumping each year seems to go from strength to strength. Great moments of one year are quickly forgotten before the end of another : yet many are worth recalling. It is these that I have attempted to recall in this book.

Chapter 1: *The 1952 Olympics*

'Never, never, never give in' – the advice given to young Harrovians by Sir Winston Churchill, visiting his old school during the war surely sums up the dramatic finale to the Helsinki Olympic Games.

It started at six o'clock in the morning on Sunday, 3rd August, 1952. It was a perfect morning – even that early – and it was quite obvious that as the day developed it was going to be very hot indeed. When the British team, which consisted of Colonel Harry Llewellyn with Foxhunter, Wilf White with Nizefella and Colonel Dougie Stewart on Aherlow, walked the course, it was quite obvious that the course was extremely demanding and would be even more so when the sun was at its height in the afternoon. This, in fact, was to be very relevant as it turned out.

Any Olympic course is a big course, but in the opinion of many the Helsinki course was at that time the biggest course that had ever been built for show jumping.

In all there were forty-eight competitors and, although Britain started very hot favourites – their team never having been beaten in two years in international events – the opposition was extremely strong.

In the Olympic Games' team event one rider from each team goes; then the next rider from each team, and finally, the third. Nowadays there are four in a team, with only the best three counting, as in a Nations' Cup, but until 1972 there were only three in a team and all three counted. Each team jumps two rounds.

The first to go for Britain was Aherlow. This great Irish-bred mare faulted at the third fence, parallels, and the second combination, the double parallels, but the great, big, red wall and the gate coming immediately after the water – the fences expected to cause the most trouble – presented no difficulties for her. It was, therefore, considered highly satisfactory that Aherlow had only 8 faults.

Next to go for Britain was Nizefella. Nizefella was at his brilliant best and it was only the very last fence of all that he touched – and it literally was a touch – for 4 faults.

By the time that two horses from each team had jumped in the first round Britain was lying second, but the great Foxhunter was still to come, and it is no exaggeration to say that Foxhunter was then considered the greatest horse in the world.

However, the events that followed were nothing if not dramatic; the horse was trained to a peak but, as he came into the arena, it was obvious that he was over-fresh. He was 'peaking' as he was ridden round awaiting his turn. This was most uncharacteristic and, in fact, to those who knew the horse well, it was all too clear that he had been insufficiently 'ridden in'. But why? There was no more experienced rider than Colonel Harry Llewellyn: this surely was the greatest event of both his own life and that of his famous horse.

All too soon our worst fears were justified. At the first set of parallels Foxhunter faulted; this seemed to unbalance him and he met the wall, which was 5 ft. 3 in. high, so completely wrong that he all but stopped. Somehow, however, he made a tremendous jump – virtually from a stand – only just touching one brick, but at least getting safely to the other side.

This was 4 faults, but far worse was the position in which Colonel Llewellyn found himself. He was virtually hanging upside down and Foxhunter was still moving, so that it seemed certain that at any moment Harry Llewellyn must lose his grip, fall off – at the cost, of course, of 8 faults – and allow Foxhunter to gallop out of the arena, which would eliminate the whole team.

Harry Llewellyn, however, refused to capitulate. He struggled and struggled until eventually he was back in the saddle, but Foxhunter had jogged round during all this in a circle which added 3 faults for a refusal. He then finished up so close to the next fence that it was quite impossible for him to jump it properly, and another 4 faults were added.

This was the worst performance that anyone had ever seen Foxhunter give. At first people thought that it might be due to the rider's nerves which had communicated themselves to the horse, but nobody could believe this to be the real reason: and so it turned out.

After all these adventures Foxhunter appeared to pull himself together and he jumped the rest of the round perfectly, but the refusal and the fences down, with time faults added, meant that he had no less than $16\frac{3}{4}$ faults, which for him was scarcely believable. Even more incredible was the fact that, at the end of the first round, Foxhunter was only placed thirty-sixth out of forty-eight, and Britain, with a total score of $28\frac{3}{4}$, were only in sixth position behind the United States, Portugal, Argentina, Chile and France. It is likely that Italy, too, would have been ahead of Britain had it not been for the fact that Piero d'Inzeo incredibly missed his turn and so eliminated the whole of the Italian team.

There was a gap of three hours between the first round and the second round, and many people were of the opinion that any rider who had gone through the experience that Harry Llewellyn had – especially when he and his horse were the hot favourites for the individual title – might well have disappeared altogether and never been seen again, or even done away with himself! But Harry Llewellyn is not this sort of person. In fact, he showed incredible *savoir faire*. He put Foxhunter away, nailing up a bit of sacking over the top half of the stable door so that the horse should be undisturbed and get some rest. He himself then went back to his hotel and retired to his room, telling the hotel porter when he wanted to be awakened. In due course he returned to the stadium and started 'riding in' Foxhunter. He still believed that he would, in fact, be proved right.

And so indeed he was: for just as he had expected, the stadium at Helsinki was now like an oven. The sun at its height was bearing down into that stadium at a heat which was something in excess of 80°F.

Not altogether to the surprise of those who had really considered the situation, the horses as a whole jumped far less well than in the morning because of this oppressive heat. Aherlow however, did better than in the morning, and had only one fence down for 4 faults, so that by the end of the first horse from each nation completing the course, Britain had pulled up from sixth to third place.

Nizefella, too, jumped even better in the second round than in the first, and there is no doubt that he was the un-luckiest horse in the whole competition. Meeting every fence right, he never looked like faulting, but checked suddenly after the water to negotiate the next fence accurately, he made such a tremendous jump that poor Wilf White found himself coming to the last fence without a stirrup. But he was over and home and together with the handful of British supporters at Helsinki – and, I suspect, many, many others – he expected to hear announced the clear round that would have given him the individual gold medal.

However, it was not to be. For one of the two judges on the ground at the water jump had raised his flag, which meant that Nizefella had been given 4 faults at the water. In the opinion of most eye-witnesses the little splash made by Nizefella at the water was from the water which over-flowed the tape at the lip of the 16ft.-wide jump; it only counts as a fault if the splash is made inside the tape. Unfortunately, by the time an objection had been made, the water had been raked over and it was not possible for the judges to reverse their decision even had they wished to do so, with the result that Nizefella was robbed of the individual show jumping gold medal at Helsinki.

But there was still a chance that Britain could win the team gold medal, however slender it might seem after Foxhunter's appalling performance in the first round. Nevertheless, anxious mathematics had shown that if Foxhunter were to go clear, or even have 4 faults, then Britain could still win the gold medal. More than 4 faults and the team would be second to Chile. More than 8 faults and they would not get a medal at all.

The suspense, therefore, as Foxhunter came in for that final round late in the afternoon, in this inferno of a stadium, was tremendous. This time he had been sufficiently 'ridden in' and also, because he had not been overworked in the morning, he was looking, in comparison with most horses that had jumped, fresh, well and fit to go for his life.

As indeed, he did. The moment the bell went and he started on the course it was obvious that this was the old Foxhunter that we knew so well. Away he went, jumping each fence effortlessly; making the fences look, in fact, far less formidable than Olympic fences invariably are. Safely over the treble; safely over the big parallels; safely over the 5 ft. 3 in. wall; over the water, with inches to spare; and then the last line. The first of the remaining fences was poles over 8 ft. of water. Foxhunter jumped so big over it that he found himself out of stride for the next fence, which was an enormous set of parallels. And here the brilliance of Harry Llewellyn's horsemanship and technical ability showed themselves, for, as he rode at these huge parallels, he swung Foxhunter slightly to the right and then turned him back towards the fence, which admittedly he met at a slight angle – and already it was over 7 ft. wide – but at least he met it absolutely perfectly. He threw a huge jump and although he hit the second pole, rattling it, he did not dislodge it, and with an increasing roar from the crowd rising in a crescendo he galloped up to, and over, the last fence for a superb clear round: a clear round which had completely eclipsed the disaster of his first round, and which had ensured a gold medal for Britain.

It could so easily have been a double gold had not Nizefella been faulted at the water. As it was he had to jump-off against the clock with four others who also had a total of 4 faults. These were d'Oriola (France), Christi (Chile), Theidemann (Germany) and de Menezes (Brazil).

Nizefella was never at his best against the clock and he had no option but to go steady for a clear round. This he achieved, but unfortunately three others achieved clear rounds in faster times than his, so he was robbed altogether of an Olympic medal as far as individual jumping was concerned.

Today, with Britain so much at the top of the tree in show jumping, it is not easy to appreciate the remarkable excitement that gold medal won by the show jumpers in Helsinki in 1952 caused back at home in Britain. But it has to be remembered that, at those particular Olympic Games, Britain had not won a single medal of any sort in any event, and so with the show jumping coming at the very end of the Games – the last event of all, in fact, which is its traditional place immediately before the Closing Ceremony – it was literally a fifty-ninth minute of the eleventh hour reprieve. Thanks to the British riders and horses, Britain did not after all come back from Helsinki entirely empty-handed.

In fact, they came back to a heroes' welcome. For many people it was the first time that they had ever seriously considered show jumping as a sport, and because it was a sport at which the British could succeed, they welcomed it with open arms. The British show jumpers had greater press coverage than any other sport when the Olympic athletes returned from Helsinki. Certainly they deserved it, but the welcome that they received and the reception that they were accorded was to play a great part in the future of show jumping in this country – and perhaps in the whole world because of the influence that Britain had always wielded in show jumping circles the world over.

For the first time show jumping was a sport that attracted the limelight. For the first time a show jumper had become a household name, and people would go anywhere to see this legendary Foxhunter. Only slightly less famous – and perhaps if one really thinks about it, it should have been the other way round – Nizefella, too, made a lasting impression on the British public: one could almost say literally, because what really impressed the British public about Nizefella was the famous sledgehammer kick-back as he jumped his fences.

And so a new age was born for this comparatively new sport. Few would disagree – especially if they were privileged to be present – that the British gold medal at Helsinki, and in particular Foxhunter's final medal-clinching round – will always rank high amongst the great historic moments of show jumping: and a turning point for Britain.

Chapter II: *Foxhunter's third King George V Gold Cup*

The King George V Cup, competed for at the Royal International Horse Show, is generally accepted as the major individual show jumping competition of the world.

Up to the outbreak of the Second World War this Cup, which had been competed for since before the First World War, had only on one occasion been won by the same rider three times. That was the late Colonel Jack Talbot-Ponsonby, who was later to become famous as one of the leading course designers. On winning the Cup three times he gave it back for re-presentation. In 1939 it was won by an Italian rider, and most people feared that after the war it would never be seen again. However, with a certain amount of luck, and a great deal of hard work, the famous trophy was traced to its hideaway in Italy and was brought back to London.

The trophy itself is a magnificent gold representation of a mounted St. George slaying the legendary dragon.

Colonel Harry Llewellyn and his famous Foxhunter had already won the King George V Gold Cup on two occasions. In 1953, however – the year after their Helsinki triumph – Foxhunter had shown conspicuous lack of form. He was, therefore, rested, re-appearing halfway through the season, towards the end of June. Immediately he showed good form. At the great German show at Aachen he was placed in every competition in which he took part; in fact, during the whole week, he had only one fence down. He was now twelve years old and it was no secret that Colonel Harry Llewellyn was desperately anxious to win the King George V Gold Cup for the third time and so become the first rider ever to win it three times on the same horse.

But what a drama was to surround that great event in July 1953. The week started well with good weather and indeed, on the Wednesday of the show, both the morning and the afternoon were fine, but it is the Wednesday evening that is traditionally the gala night of the whole Royal International. As on so many other occasions, both before and since, Her Majesty the Queen and the Duke of Edinburgh were to grace the show with their presence. But as the afternoon performance came to an end ominous black clouds could be seen rolling up from the west. Was the weather going to break?

A telephone call was put through to the Meteorological Office. Yes, rain was expected – heavy showers all through the evening. There was, however, a possibility that they would pass north of London.

At about half past five it suddenly became so dark that it might well have been night and an ominous patter-patter could be heard on the roof of the marquee, in which the stewards and officials of the show were having their tea. Within seconds rather than minutes the downpour was torrential; indeed it could almost be described as tropical. For fifteen minutes at least it was physically impossible to leave the tent as the rain made a great sheet of water outside the entrance.

The storm lasted just forty minutes, but in that forty minutes it had reduced the famous stadium at the White City from a green-turfed centre with a red running track surrounding it to a lake. The whole stadium was awash.

What was going to happen? Would the whole show be cancelled? Would the start be postponed? Would the performances carry on, hoping that the water would drain away in what was now little more than an hour before the gala evening performance started with the arrival of the Queen?

A hurried consultation was held. I remember donning

gumboots and wading out into the arena with Colonel Mike Ansell, the Show Director. We discussed the situation, considered every possibility. We sought the advice of other people closely concerned – officials, the White City ground staff, the General Manager, some of the riders, the judges and stewards. Everybody gave their own advice and finally, at about twenty minutes past six, Colonel Ansell made his decision.

'The show will go on.' It was as though that brave decision and the announcement which I was asked to make over the public address system to inform the many people who were also waiting to hear was to affect the very weather itself. Almost immediately the skies cleared, the last few drops of rain that had still been felt since the storm passed disappeared, and suddenly there was a clear sky above us and a brisk wind led us to hope that there would be no further storm that evening.

And so it turned out. The show started on time. The Queen and the Duke of Edinburgh arrived and took their places in the Royal Box and miraculously the flood water disappeared from the arena, except for more low-lying parts of the running track.

The great feature of the 1953 show was the first appearance in London of the famous Lippizaner stallions from the Spanish Riding School of Vienna. They gave their display despite the conditions and immediately afterwards there was the parade of the twenty-four competitors for the King George V Gold Cup. Darkness was falling and the great stadium lights were switched on. A hush descended on the crowd as the first horse came in to jump.

There were fifteen fences in the King George V Gold Cup that year and the course was considered big but fair, the most difficult fence apparently being a double oxer with a very big spread. In fact, each of the first five horses were to fault at this fence, including the great Nizefella. People began to wonder whether this fence was jumpable. Was there going to be a repetition of the previous year when only two horses out of twenty-four starters cleared the water? But then Michael Tubridy came in on Red Castle, for Ireland, and having negotiated the big spread, completed a clear round.

A few minutes later there was another clear round and again it was from Ireland – O'Shea on Kilcarne. Then came in a seven-year old horse which had yet to make its reputation – Merano, ridden by Raimondo d'Inzeo. Clear! There were now only three more to jump and still there was no clear round for Britain, but Foxhunter had yet to come.

He entered the arena with great confidence, took measure of the course, jumped it perfectly and there was a clear round for the famous gold medallists. But the last horse to go – yet another from Ireland – also went clear. Kevin Barry on Ballynonty. Barry had won the King George V Gold Cup two years earlier; Llewellyn and Foxhunter had won the cup twice.

And so to the jump-off. Five were involved – three from Ireland, one from Italy and one from Great Britain. Red Castle went first and was clear again. Kilcarne had 12 faults. Merano, already showing something of her brilliance, nevertheless just touched a brick at the wall and dislodged it: 4 faults. Now it was Foxhunter's turn. Riding rather more slowly, a little more deliberately this time, Harry Llewellyn took him round the course, only accelerating at the big spread. He cleared it, checked as he approached the wall, was clear again, and meeting the last fence absolutely right – a big double – he was safely over that and home for a second clear round.

There was a storm of applause as all the pent-up emotion created not only by the suspense of the competition but of the storm drama preceding the evening, was released.

'You can breathe again now,' I said over the loudspeaker system and one could almost feel the sudden relaxation. The mighty Foxhunter was still in with a chance. In fact, there was one more to go in that first jump-off, but Ballynonty, obviously tiring, proved no great threat to Foxhunter, for he had 12 faults.

The judges decided that there should be a short break before the final jump-off as, the going being so heavy and sticky, it was obvious that the horses were finding it a great effort to jump. Eventually, with the fences raised, many of them now standing at over 5 ft. 6 in., the signal was given for the jump-off to start. The tension was now almost unbearable. I can seldom remember a greater atmosphere created at the Royal International.

Red Castle had to go first. He appeared to be jumping as well as ever, but on this occasion the big spread was too much for him and he had the second pole down. And then, at the one-but-last fence, he made a careless mistake and so finished the round with 8 faults.

What a chance for Foxhunter! Surely he could not fail us now – though obviously there were some who still remembered that first round at Helsinki and appreciated the fact that a horse is not a machine.

Foxhunter entered the arena to a great burst of spontaneous applause; then there was absolute silence while Colonel Llewellyn waited for the bell to signal him to start.

'Now you can hear a pin drop, but let's hope it won't be a pole.' Such was the tension that, even as commentator sitting out there in my commentary position in the middle of the arena, it was impossible not to be affected by it.

The bell went and Foxhunter started. He looked superb, supremely confident; one only hoped that his rider was feeling as confident as the horse looked. Over the first, over the second: he touched a brick at the great, red wall and it was down – 4 faults, and still five fences to go, including the two biggest on the course. The suspense was unbearable. He came to the treble – safely over. Only one fence to go – the double. Over – one stride – over again, and Foxhunter finished the round with only 4 faults, and thus was the winner of the King George V Gold Cup for the third time. Everyone was on his feet. People were cheering and waving their handkerchiefs. Foxhunter once again was the great hero of the occasion.

This, without doubt, was Foxhunter's finest hour. If ever there had been any doubt that his reputation would last as long as show jumping itself, this competition was to immortalise him, for he became the first horse ever to win the King George V Gold Cup three times. In fact, since then, Piero d'Inzeo and David Broome have both won the King George V Gold Cup on three occasions, but neither of them on the same horse. D'Inzeo won first on Uruguay and then twice on The Rock. David Broome won on three different horses – on Sunsalve, on Mister Softee and on Sportsman, but Llewellyn had won it on each occasion on the one great horse, Foxhunter.

That was really the peak of Foxhunter's career. A few weeks later he won the national championship and became the first horse to win both the national championship and what could be described as the international championship. At the end of the season, at the Horse of the Year Show at Harringay, he made a mistake at a double in a comparatively unimportant competition. He caught the pole between his two forelegs and it brought him down. After this he seemed rather to lose his confidence and I do not believe that we ever really saw the great Foxhunter again. Not very long afterwards Harry Llewellyn decided to retire this great horse and when, a few years later, he died, his skeleton was given to the National Equine Research Station at Newmarket, while his head and hide were buried in the mountains above Colonel Llewellyn's home: without doubt, one of the immortals.

Chapter III: *The Immortal Sunsalve*

Unlike the Olympic Games in Helsinki and Stockholm, the equestrian events in Rome were held in two parts. There was an individual jumping Grand Prix and a team event, or Nations' Cup. It was in the team event that one of the most spectacular rounds I ever remember occurred. It concerned David Broome and that great horse owned by Elizabeth Anderson called Sunsalve. This horse, a big, raw-boned chestnut, by Skoiter, was one of the strongest horses I have ever seen, or indeed known, for I had the privilege of riding it myself when, as a four-year-old, it was shown at the Norfolk County Show. It was, in fact, no show horse and I was only able to place it fourth in its class, but I was so impressed by the ride that, at the end of the judging, I asked Elizabeth Anderson whether the horse was for sale. She told me it was and that her father, who had bred the horse and really owned it, was asking £600. In those days, this was a very high price for a hunter and I told her that it was just about twice what I expected to pay; but she assured me that her father would take no less so I thought no more about it.

I very quickly remembered the horse when first I saw it jumping and it was no surprise to me when Elizabeth Anderson, on Sunsalve, won the Queen Elizabeth Cup.

Elizabeth, however, would be the first to admit that the horse was really too strong for her, and that inevitably there would be occasions when she found herself unable to steady it and so collect unnecessary faults, and indeed a few very unpleasant-looking falls. Accordingly, David Broome was invited to ride it, and he immediately established a rapport between himself and the horse which led them very quickly to become an outstanding international combination.

It was no surprise to anyone when David and Sunsalve were selected to represent Britain in the Rome Olympic Games in 1960.

The unforgettable round took place in the team event, but it is worth first mentioning an incident in the individual event in which David Broome won his first bronze medal. (He was to win a second one in Mexico on Mister Softee.)

The course for the individual Grand Prix was very big and it was made bigger by the decision of the Technical Delegate to alter slightly the distances in the treble. It was difficult for a rider to decide whether to take one stride or two strides between the second and third elements. To try and take only one stride made it almost impossible to reach easily the third element which consisted of parallel poles, yet there was scarcely enough room to put in a second stride. The result was that horse after horse, during the first round, faulted at the treble; many of them having bad falls, including the great Meteor, ridden by the famous German rider Fritz Theidemann: in fact I never remember Meteor falling on any other occasion.

David Broome, on Sunsalve, was one of those who attempted to take only one stride between the second and third elements, but he crashed through the poles, thus collecting 4 faults. Between the two rounds I saw David and said that I supposed he would not attempt to take only one stride in the second round.

'Oh yes,' he said, 'I am quite sure that I can do it.' Asked why he had failed in the first round, he said it was because as he turned into it the sun was behind him and shone very brilliantly on the newly-painted red wall which was the first element of the treble. Sunsalve, suddenly seeing this glaring newly-painted wall, slightly lost his impulsion, and so could not reach easily the third element in one stride after the parallels in the middle.

28

'But later this afternoon,' David added confidently, 'the sun will have gone right round and I am quite sure that we can make it.'

He did. And thanks to this great exhibition of jumping he won the individual bronze medal.

In the team event the course was even bigger, and again there was a massive treble, which came quite early on in the course. One of the team – Franco (still going strong in 1973, ridden by Caroline Bradley) – the mount of David Barker, found it impossible to reach the third element, again a big spread, and stopped. David took him round for a second attempt, but he stopped again. At the third attempt he made it, but had the second and third elements down. He then jumped perfectly until he came to the very last fence. To reach this fence one passed the entrance to the collecting ring and then swung away to jump the final parallels.

Franco at that time was not very experienced – and there was criticism, though probably it was not entirely justified, that the team manager had made a mistake in not letting Franco jump in the individual event in order to get the necessary experience. He probably allowed his concentration to wander, and thinking of the collecting ring he dodged out. This virtually eliminated the British team, because at one time it was announced that no team that had had an elimination in the first round would be allowed to jump again in the second round. However, when it came to the second round, in the afternoon, there was an announcement to the effect that every team could jump, but that any horse that had been eliminated would be given a score equal to the worst round of the whole competition plus twenty.

And so the second round, as far as Britain was concerned, was really only of academic interest. Nevertheless, it produced one of the greatest, most exciting and ultimately most frustrating rounds that I ever remember.

Halfway round the course there was a water jump 16 ft. wide. The next fence was parallel poles, but to reach it one had to turn very sharp to the left after the water jump, at an angle of 90°. Most riders found that if they cleared the water, which they could only do by getting up a tremendous speed, then they could not turn to the left in a sufficiently balanced manner to be able to negotiate the big set of parallels. So either they risked 4 faults at the water and then turned easily to the parallels, or they attempted to clear the water knowing that they would either have to miss the parallels altogether, because they could not get round in time, or meet the parallels so unbalanced that they were bound to have them down.

Horse after horse, in the second round, faulted at the water and, as each horse went in, the judge sitting by the side of the water raised his flag to signal to the judges in their box at the top of the stand, that the horse had faulted. When it came to Sunsalve's turn he was in his greatest form, and jumped round the huge Olympic course like a galleon in full sail. He swept down to the water jump and cleared it by at least eighteen inches. His jump and his clearance of the water which had caused so much trouble was so spectacular that, commenting for television, I actually said, 'Well, they can't put up the flag for that!'

Superb horseman that he is, David then just touched the reins with the very lightest contact on Sunsalve's mouth – to ride this horse he used a very severe bridle, but with his superb independent seat, his balance and his beautiful hands, he never hurt Sunsalve in the slightest, despite the severity of the bit – and turned, completely collected, for the parallels. Safely over, he swung on to the rest of the course. He never faulted, making it look almost childishly easy.

As he swung away from the collecting ring and effortlessly cleared the last fence, a tremendous cheer went up. In fact, as he rode from the arena, a crowd approaching 100,000 rose to their feet and cheered him all the way out of the stadium – the only clear round of the Olympic Games in 1960.

It was an unforgettable moment and it made one very proud to be associated with the British team, despite the disasters of the morning round. Yet tragedy and disappointment were to follow, for, as the next horse was halfway round, I noticed out of the corner of my eye the nought on the great electric scoreboard at the end of the arena changed to four.

How on earth, I wondered, could they have given Sunsalve 4 faults? It must surely be a mistake. But no. Sunsalve had 4 faults, and so was denied that great clear round.

What happened? It seems that the judge at the water had seen a splash as Sunsalve landed, and for a moment thought that he must have dropped a foot in the water, and so he raised the flag. He then realised that Sunsalve was well clear and realised that, in all probability, the splash was made by turf being kicked back into the water and so he dropped his flag.

It so happened, however, that Prince Bernhard of the Netherlands, then President of the International Federation, was in the ring at the time. He went across to the judge and asked if he knew what the rules were, and in case he did not, reminded him that the water jump judge could not alter his decision for an infringement at the water without reference to the full jury and, as he had raised his flag, it must stand as a fault unless the jury agreed otherwise.

As the overall result was in no way affected, it was obviously irrelevant to refer the matter to the jury and so Sunsalve's 4 faults were allowed to stand.

It was, of course, of no real importance because the result did not involve Britain. It would have been had the team event and the individual event been jumped as one competition, as was the case at Helsinki and Stockholm. Britain was already too far behind in the team event to come into the reckoning, and so there was no point in querying the water judge's decision.

Nevertheless, it has always seemed to me very sad that

Sunsalve was denied the glory of the only Olympic clear round in Rome, and furthermore, it has always seemed to me that those who saw that round saw one of the greatest rounds in all Olympic show jumping.

Oddly enough, David himself did not know the true explanation of those 4 faults until I told him myself in a Grandstand programme at the Horse of the Year Show 1972, but that is typical of David; he is never concerned with the past or the future, but is just concerned with getting on with the present: and not over-seriously with that. His is surely the ideal temperament for any international sportsman, and there can be little doubt that this temperament has played its part in winning him World and European Championships.

Chapter IV: *David and Goliath*

The first occasion on which show jumping was televised was at the Olympic Games at Wembley in 1948, but I have always thought that it was a competition at the Horse of the Year Show in 1950 – the second Horse of the Year Show at Harringay – which really persuaded the public that show jumping was one of the most 'tele-photogenic' of all sports.

The event to which I am referring was the Puissance competition that year for the Fred Foster Cup, and when finally the course was reduced, as usual, to two great fences, there were only two horses left in the competition. One was the mighty Foxhunter, ridden, of course, by Colonel Harry Llewellyn, and although it was more than two years since their Olympic triumph at Helsinki, they were still the most famous equestrian partnership in the world. The other was a little mare called Finality, ridden by a young rider barely twenty years old, called Pat Smythe. This was her first show jumper. She had, in fact, bought this little mare, whose mother pulled a milk float, for very little money near her Gloucestershire home. But, although only 15 h.h. this mare, thanks to the brilliant training and riding of Pat Smythe, quickly established herself as one of the best jumpers in the country, and only three months after Pat had first jumped it, she had had the honour to represent Britain at Ostend.

Unfortunately, Pat had been unable to afford to refuse the generous offer made for Finality by a north-countryman – about £1,000! – and so she sold her, but in a new stable, with a different rider, the mare achieved no success. So at the first Horse of the Year Show, Pat Smythe was invited to

B

ride her again. Immediately she won the Leading Show Jumper of the Year championship.

Now, twelve months later, she found herself in this final jump-off with Colonel Llewellyn and Foxhunter in the Puissance, a David and Goliath situation if ever there was one. Foxhunter stood nearly 17 h.h.; his rider an Olympic Gold Medallist. Finality was little more than a pony – her rider barely out of her teens.

Finality had to jump first. The wall stood at over 6 ft. The first fence was a huge triple bar with a spread of nearly 7 ft. Finality jumped this fence awkwardly, but carefully. She turned at the end of the arena, sailed down to the wall and cleared that too.

It was then Foxhunter's turn. He jumped first the triple bar and then the wall – both clear. Both fences were then raised. Little Finality came in again. She met the triple awkwardly again and, although she made a great jump screwing over it, she had a pole down. She then turned to jump the big wall and, again, only just got over this: 4 faults. This seemed to be handing it to Foxhunter. He sailed down to the triple and jumped as though it were nothing at all, but turning to the wall he appeared to be a little over-confident, jumped it carelessly and, just tapping a brick, it came down, to give him 4 faults, and so they were equal once again.

The fences were raised. There was an absolute hush as the diminutive Finality and the youthful Pat Smythe rode into the ring. She galloped down to the triple bar, screwed over it, landing well to the left-hand side, but she was clear. Then Pat Smythe did a truly remarkable thing. She pulled up Finality altogether, and there were many people who thought that she had decided that the big, red wall was too much and that she was therefore going to retire. But not at all. In fact, she was just giving her little mare a brief opportunity to get properly balanced. She turned at the end of the arena to face the wall, gathered the reins, applied the pressure of her legs to Finality's sides and set off towards this great wall. She only cleared it by an inch or two, just rapping it with the hind hooves, but she *was* clear. And so, to keep in the competition, the great Foxhunter had to go clear again as well.

He came in looking every inch the greatest show jumper in the world – as undoubtedly he then was. He jumped the triple bar safely, and this time Colonel Harry Llewellyn was allowing no careless mistake at the wall. He collected himself, measured his stride, drove forward and cleared the wall.

And so both were clear yet again. There was a pause. The atmosphere in the stadium was by this time as tense as only these great occasions can inspire. Some eight thousand people awaited the appearance of Finality for yet another jump-off.

At this moment the telephone at my commentary position (which is also the control point at the Horse of the Year Show) rang. My assistant picked up the telephone and then whispered something to me. I was asked to make an announcement. But I did nothing. There was a few moments' pause and then my assistant whispered to me, 'You were told to give it out.' But I declined. I felt that what I was asked to announce could, in fact, be made public in a far more dramatic way. Instead, therefore, I gave the signal to open the gates from the collecting ring into the arena.

The gates were opened and into the arena rode the mighty Foxhunter – nearly 17 h.h. – and by his side the little Finality –the David and Goliath that had been thrilling the crowd for the last half hour. When they reached the centre of the arena I gave another signal and the 'boxing lights' were switched on, bathing the whole of the centre of that famous arena in a bright amber light. At that moment Harry Llewellyn leant down and offered his hand to Pat Smythe, who took it. Before that vast crowd they shook hands and Harry Llewellyn took off his hat to Pat.

That gesture made it quite clear that they had decided

to divide. Another jump-off would mean that they would either equal yet again when already they had jumped quite enough, or one would have to be the loser when neither deserved to lose, so they had decided they would be equal first.

I do not think that I have ever heard a cheer the likes of that one which went up in the Harringay Stadium at that second Horse of the Year Show until 1972– an incident which I will describe in a later chapter.

The cheering continued for several minutes as Foxhunter and Finality, and their gallant riders, stayed there in the centre of the arena. Finally, to continuing applause, they rode out, to come back a few minutes later for the presentation of the trophy and the rosettes.

Already it was nearly midnight. As far as television was concerned we had overrun by more than an hour, but I very much doubt if more than a handful of viewers had switched off, for during the last two hours, they had had something that had turned out to be absolutely compulsive viewing – perhaps for the very first time as far as show jumping was concerned.

For more than two hours the telephones were ringing. Viewers were telephoning the Harringay Stadium, the Horse of the Year Show office, the b.b.c., even my own home, to say what fantastic viewing they had enjoyed. I have little doubt that it was this great competition, which had so caught the imagination not only of the spectators present but of the millions of viewers watching at home, that was to make the b.b.c. appreciate to the full the possibility of show jumping as a television sport.

More than that, honour was satisfied in every way. The great hero, Colonel Harry Llewellyn, and his immortal Foxhunter had certainly not been disgraced, but Cinderella in the shape of Pat Smythe with her little mare Finality, had given them a very good run for their money, and had finished on equal terms. This, to the general public, was a fairy-tale ending that could satisfy even the most romantic.

Not surprisingly from that moment onwards, Pat Smythe became the darling of the British public. Today few remember her gallant little mare, Finality – which at that time, of course, was no longer her own property. She not only consolidated but enhanced her reputation with her famous mare, Tosca, bought for a few pounds from a draft that came over from Ireland and whose breeding was unknown, and her equally famous Prince Hal, which also she bought for a comparatively low sum of money, having seen it run unsuccessfully in a selling hurdle at Cheltenham.

There could hardly have been two more dissimilar horses than Tosca and Prince Hal yet, for the following three years, Pat Smythe on these horses was the leading rider in Britain. In 1956 she was to become the first lady rider ever to represent her country in the equestrian events of the Olympic Games. She was then riding Flanagan – a horse originally brought out as a three-day event horse and ridden at Badminton by his owner, Brigadier Bolton. It was then bought by that great patron of show jumping, Mr Robert Hanson, who originally bought this great Irish-bred horse for his son, William Hanson, who tragically died less than a year later.

Bob Hanson then invited Pat Smythe to ride his horse and at the end of its career he gave it to her. Meanwhile it had achieved just about everything that a show jumper could be asked to achieve and indeed, although it was not really an Olympic horse, Pat had ridden it and been far from disgraced in two Olympic Games.

Chapter V: *The Lighter Side*

Although for the most part one associates show jumping with drama and highly dramatic incidents, yet from time to time there is a lighter side. I can recall many amusing incidents over the last twenty or more years, but there is one that stands out in my memory.

It was in 1956, in a Gambler's Competition, at the Horse of the Year Show. In this particular competition each fence had a large playing-card attached. There were twelve fences in the ring, but only seven had to be jumped and the competitors chose for themselves which seven they would jump. Obviously the more difficult fences carried the higher-scoring cards – and the greater risk. The easier fences were only sixes and sevens and eights.

The most difficult fence of all was a big treble running down the centre of the arena, consisting of just three single poles. This fence carried the ace, and if one negotiated it successfully, one scored thirteen points.

In 1956, in a competition like this, the riders could jump any fence any number of times, but only seven fences in all: if they had a fence down they had to jump a different fence, but could return to the original fence immediately afterwards. Nowadays the rule has been altered and generally a rider is only allowed to jump one fence once – or at most, twice.

At that time there was a very popular short-tailed horse called Nugget. He was a Welsh Cob and a great personality, immensely popular with the crowd wherever he appeared. He was ridden by John Walmsley.

John knew from experience that this horse just had to be

left to himself; it was a waste of time to try and put him right, but if left alone he could adjust his stride and jump the most prodigious obstacles.

When Nugget came in nobody had scored the maximum, which was, of course, seven times thirteen. John Walmsley wasted no time and went straight for the big treble. Down the line he went faultlessly, John riding on a completely loose rein. He turned at the end of the arena, three or four strides, and off he went again, clearing the treble a second time. A turn at the end and he attacked it for the third time; and so he continued, sometimes getting so close to the second or third element that it seemed as though he took about six strides between the two elements, rather than the two which had been anticipated by the course builder. But then, at about the fifth attempt, he hit the third part of the treble and down it came. So he jumped the king – for twelve points – and then, the pole having been put up again, back he went to the treble!

By this time everyone was in hysterics. They had completely lost count, and the style of Nugget's jumping had not only the packed arena at Harringay in fits of laughter but several million viewers at home : and to be honest, the Commentator.

Eventually he had jumped his seven fences and retired with a score of seventy-seven.

The next rider to come in was Seamus Hayes, on a horse called Waving Corn. He knew that the rules included one to the effect that if a competitor knocked down part of a combination, he then had to go back and jump the whole thing again, and in this competition it was only a fence *cleared* that amassed points; there were no faults for a refusal or a fall. He therefore employed the same tactics as Nugget, but whenever he hit a part of the combination he made his horse stop at the next part, dashed back to the start, held up his hand to show the judges he was ready to begin as soon as the fence was re-built, and they had rung the bell.

In this way his seven fences seemed endless, but he carried on, frequently faulting at the first or second part of the treble, and then stopping at the second or third, and so collecting no faults, but still collecting a maximum of thirteen each time he actually jumped the complete treble.

This went on and on for minutes and the laughter was no less than it had been for Nugget. In fact, I can honestly say that I do not remember any serious show jumping event at an important show receiving such a hilarious reception – except perhaps when Harvey Smith took the bareback riding competition at the Royal International Horse Show 1972 a little too literally and actually removed his shirt! At last Seamus Hayes finished and, to roars of applause and cascades of laughter, he rode out of the arena waving cheerfully to the crowd, but just as he got to the exit the score was announced. There was a sudden silence as the audience listened to it. But what an anti-climax! Seamus had been disqualified! Apparently he himself had lost count of the number of times that he had cleared the fence and so, when the judges added it all up, they found that he had jumped the fence once too often and so he had jumped a total of more than seven fences in all. The judges had no option but to disqualify him.

For the record, it was old Nizefella who eventually won the competition.

Nugget was immensely popular in the comparatively short time during which he was at the top of the tree: and John Walmsley was the ideal partner for him. Seamus Hayes will always, I think, be considered as one of the great personalities of show jumping. In the early days he was at his greatest in speed events, many of his duels with Alan Oliver being quite unforgettable. Later he reached the very apex of his career on that great Irish-bred horse, Goodbye, again and again having the hearts of the audience in their mouths as he pulled off superb feats of jumping, particularly over really big fences. One can but hope that in the not-too-distant future, he will again have horses of top international standard.

For personalities such as Seamus Hayes are much needed in any sport, and his absence from the principal international shows leaves show jumping the poorer.

Chapter VI: *European Championship*

The European Championship is usually held alternately with the World Championship, but every other year, while the World Championship is held every four years. Although the details of its conditions are usually left to the host country the pattern is generally the same : a series of qualifiers with a final for the best placed horses.

Over the years there have been some good competitions, not surprisingly the same names usually being associated with the climax – Winkler, Alwin Schockemöhle, Piero and Raimondo d'Inzeo, Broome. There are, however, two occasions which stand out in my memory, both of which took place in England.

The first was at the Royal International Horse Show at the White City in 1963. It was surely one of the least successful Royal Internationals. To begin with the weather was appalling throughout, the ring quickly becoming a quagmire. Secondly, to include the European Championship competitions in a programme which was already packed with traditional annual events of major importance – such as the King George V Gold Cup, the John Player Trophy, the Prince of Wales Cup, the Queen Elizabeth Cup, the Lonsdale Trophy, the Horse and Hound Cup – created great difficulties. Inevitably leading riders concerned in the European Championship boycotted the more traditional events.

However, despite all the problems it developed into a really first-class competition, one moreover which had a heightened interest for the British public through circumstances which might be described sympathetic and patriotic.

As so often on other occasions the Germans dominated the competition. Britain produced only one finalist. This, unexpectedly, was David Barker. In fact, he qualified both his horses, Franco and Mister Softee.

David Barker is an exceptionally fine horseman and had a wonderfully successful show jumping career, though he made no secret of the fact that the rough and tumble of the show jumping circuit was not really for him. He preferred the hunting field, the thoroughbred – breeding, schooling and dealing – in that order. There is no doubt, too, that being an extremely sensitive person despite his rugged Yorkshire background, he was very much hurt by his failure in the 1960 Olympics when Franco was eliminated in the team event. This was due in all probability to the fact that the trainer had insisted on keeping this brilliant young horse too much in cotton wool, so that he was lacking essential experience in big international jumping. He was not even allowed to jump in the individual event in Rome on the preceding Wednesday: an experience that might well have been invaluable to him. Instead the reserve combination Dawn Palethorpe and Hollandia were included, while David Broome jumped Sunsalve and won a Bronze Medal.

David Barker was to be further upset by having O'Malley taken away from him and given to Harvey Smith to ride; and finally he lost both Mister Softee to David Broome and Franco to Caroline Bradley.

Since the Rome débacle things had seldom gone well for David. He had good horses but somehow the big events consistently eluded him. No one expected anything very wonderful for him in the European Championship, yet when it came to the final he was there with both his horses qualified. Despite the fact that Franco had qualified top, David elected to ride Mister Softee – undoubtedly a wise decision.

The conditions for that final event were appalling. Eventually it narrowed down to a duel between David Barker and the inevitable Alwin Schockemöhle, against the clock. David went first and did a really brilliant round, but in such dreadful going the time was not all that fast.

Alwin Schockemöhle really decided to have a go, and although it was before the days of an easily-seen automatic clock ticking away in the centre of the arena, it did seem that he was moving the faster. He was really riding for his life. Riding like hell for the last fence, which was 15 ft. of water, he met it wrong, stood off a full stride too far back and landed himself with one of the most dramatic falls that I have ever seen.

Naturally the fall clinched the Championship for David Barker: and an extremely popular win it was. Certainly it was the climax of David's career, which was not to last very much longer. Prior to the Mexico Olympics he produced a horse which really did appear to be of Olympic calibre. Inevitably he was offered a very big price for it, but he wanted it to be available for Britain, hopefully for him to ride himself.

'Stall, by asking them double,' he was advised. Which he did and his price was immediately accepted! He could not possibly refuse and so one more good horse was lost to Britain. Ironically, as in so many instances, it has hardly been heard of since.

Curiously enough Alwin Schockemöhle was involved in the other memorable European Championship. This was at Hickstead in 1969.

The whole event began with the sort of controversy that is not alien to Hickstead, not altogether unknown in show jumping generally: and certainly not a stranger to the character most involved in the controversy, Harvey Smith.

In Rotterdam in 1967 David Broome had won the European Championship with Harvey Smith as runner-up. Despite all the ups and downs in their careers these two have usually been considered the two leading British riders in the international field. It was, therefore, something of a sensation when Harvey Smith was omitted from the selected British pair. His place was taken by Alan Oliver who, despite his brilliance, his professionalism, his consistency over more than twenty years, has never been at his best in international competition. Indeed he has probably less international experience and certainly less international success than any other leading British rider.

Now he was preferred to Harvey Smith, though there were many who felt that his two horses, Sweep and Pitz Palu, had sizeable chinks in their armour. The former had never been wholly consistent, the latter was alleged to have taken a violent dislike to Hickstead.

In 1969 there was betting at Hickstead. Ladbrokes made, not surprisingly, Schockemöhle favourite at 3–1, with Winkler 7–2 and Broome third favourite at 5–1. (Betting at Hickstead, or indeed anywhere else connected with show jumping, was short-lived, being frowned on by the F.E.I. and the B.S.J.A., and providing only minimal attraction for punters.)

In the first event, however, David's horse Mister Softee was at his very greatest. Despite the fact that it was a speed event and Mister Softee had a fence down, which meant that he had to add a five-second penalty to his time, he was still nevertheless the fastest in the class, beating Schockemöhle and Wimpel by more than two seconds.

This was a good start for Britain : but the second day was to be dramatic in the extreme. Both Oliver's horses failed over a Nations' Cup-type course, and to the astonishment and dismay of all Alan decided to withdraw his horses from the Championship altogether and return home : a move which earned him much criticism, though probably the mistake was in his ever being selected in the first place. David Broome was left on his own. Not surprisingly, the pressure told on him and at the end of the second event he had dropped behind the two Germans who now found themselves lying equal first.

Seven horses were involved in the final, but it was obvious that the real battle lay between the two German aces, Winkler and Schockemöhle, and David Broome. The Germans were riding Enigk and Donald Rex respectively. The former had been Winkler's 1968 Olympic mount. Donald Rex was considered by many the best show jumper in the world.

Of the three, David Broome had to go first and he coaxed an immaculate clear out of Mister Softee. Winkler had one fence down on Enigk. Donald Rex produced his almost inevitable clear. The suspense before the final round was tantalising : the tension when it started was electric. David was first to go again. Softee, now so at home over the course, produced another perfect clear.

Everything finally depended on Schockemöhle and the mighty Donald Rex. As at the White City four years earlier the sporting German threw everything to the wind, determined to lower the British flag and to take the European Championship once again back to Germany. He flew round that great course with its wide open spaces, attacking every fence as if he would eat it. All went well until he turned for the last line of fences. Slightly unbalanced he flattened at the first set of poles, and they were gone. The next fence was down too, and it was David Broome European Champion once again, with the one and only Mister Softee once again the winner's mount.

As so often before, and since, David Broome had risen to the really big occasion, proving himself to be one of the really great show jumping competitors. A worthy champion in fact – World or European or National.

Chapter VII: *World Championship*

A show jumping event that was quite different, and of particular interest, was held at Aachen in 1956. This was the newly-styled World Championship – now held every four years and arranged in such a way as not to coincide with the Olympic year.

At Aachen it was decided to hold this Championship in a form entirely different from the previous Championships. Only two horses and riders were allowed to enter from any one nation : a preliminary round was jumped, and the leading four then went through to the final. The unique aspect of this World Championship was that each of the four riders then had to do one round on each of the four horses : this was the first time that this form of competition had been held.

In 1956 the four finalists were Raimondo d'Inzeo on Merano, Fritz Theidemann on Meteor, Pasco Goyoaga on Fahnenkonig and Delius on Discutido. So there was one Italian-bred horse, two German-bred horses and an Argentinian-bred horse, the riders coming from Italy, Germany, Spain and the Argentine.

There was a draw for the order in which they jumped and it was Discutido who went first, ridden by his own rider, Delius. He incurred 4 faults; the next three all had clear rounds, but d'Inzeo, going a little over-cautiously, collected half a time fault.

So at the end of the first round there was really very little in it. Before the next round each rider was allowed three minutes to get used to his new horse and a practice fence was put up in the arena for the new rider to jump if he wished to. Delius now rode Fahnenkonig, and incurred 4 faults at the treble – the same fence, in fact, at which he had

47

faulted on his own horse, Discutido; so after the second round Delius had 8 faults.

Goyoaga then came in on the famous Italian mare, Merano, but just when he seemed to be going well and confidently the mare stopped at a big set of parallel poles at the top of the arena. Raimondo d'Inzeo then came in on the famous Meteor – a horse which had been considered the best in Germany for a number of years and which had been involved in one of the most exciting King George V Gold Cups at the Royal International Horse Show, when Meteor and Red Admiral, ridden by Alan Oliver, were locked in a most exciting duel which took them to three jumps-off; Meteor finally running out the winner.

He all but 'run out' in a different way in the World Championship at Aachen; there was a wall 5 ft. 6 in. high and it seemed as though he was certain to miss the jump, but in the nick of time, d'Inzeo pulled him round and, although he had to jump the wall at an angle of 45°, he cleared it and went on to repeat a clear round. This put d'Inzeo in a very strong position, having had only half a time fault in the first round.

However, Theidemann was also clear on the Argentinian Discutido and so it was he who led at the end of the second round. In the third round Theidemann, now riding Fahnenkonig, a German-bred horse, and therefore, probably the type of horse that he was used to, and Delius on Merano, both faulted at the 5 ft. parallels, while Goyoaga on Meteor – and what a perfect rapport was immediately established between them – and d'Inzeo with the impetuous little Discutido – he barely stood 15.1 h.h. – were clear.

With the scores so close the fourth round was, of course, intensely exciting. The actual scores were:

Delius	–	12
Theidemann	–	4
Goyoaga	–	3
d'Inzeo	–	$\frac{1}{2}$

SHIPS THAT PASS IN THE NIGHT
Above: Pat Smythe, who rode in the Olympics for the last time in 1960, on the dashing Prince Hal. *Below:* David Broome who rode in his first Olympics at Rome in 1960, on the spectacular Sunsalve

INTERNATIONAL IMMORTALS: *Above:* Hans Winkler, Olympic Individual Gold Medallist in 1956, on Enigk. *Below:* Bill Steinkraus, Olympic Individual Gold Medallist in 1968, on First Boy.

Above: Raimondo d'Inzeo, Olympic Individual Gold Medallist in 1960, on Merano. *Below:* Piero d'Inzeo, holder of four Olympic medals, on The Rock.

UNFORGETTABLE CHARACTERS
Above: Wilf White on the first and greatest of the famous
"kick-backs", Nizefela. *Below:* Seamus Hayes, the "darlin'"
of early Horse of the Year Shows, on Goodbye

There was less than a fence down between the first two, and one fence down covering the first three.

It was Discutido's turn to go first and he was ridden by Goyoaga, who incidentally had won the World Championship four years earlier. He did a brilliant clear round and so finished with a total of three. Then Fritz Theidemann came in on Merano, an Italian thorough-bred from the famous stud where Ribot stood, and as different as one could possibly imagine from his own Meteor. Nevertheless, by superb horsemanship, Theidemann got him round for a clear round, which gave him a total of four. Delius then rode in on Meteor and had one fence down: it was, in fact, Meteor's only fence down in the whole competition, but it meant that Delius finished with the worst score of the competition.

All now rested with Raimondo d'Inzeo, who even then in 1956, was a show jumping hero all over the world and had won a silver medal at the Stockholm Olympics a few weeks earlier. When he came to start his round his score was half a fault. His ride for this last round was the German-bred Fahnenkonig, who had previously had faults at both the treble and the big set of parallels.

With superb self-confidence Raimondo virtually ignored the three minutes allowed him to get used to his new horse. He quickly hopped over the schooling fence and went straight to the start. As on his own Merano, he began very carefully, very cautiously; he got too close to awkward parallels but somehow he extricated himself without faulting. He was over the triple bar, sailed over the three elements of the big treble, met the 5 ft. 6 in. wall perfectly and galloped through the finishing beam for a clear round, but the applause from that massive crowd at Aachen – massive despite heavy rain – was subdued because it had been quite obvious that, if his round on his own Merano had been over the time allowed, then his round on Fahnenkonig had been considerably slower. His lead was only $2\frac{1}{2}$ faults which, translated into time, meant ten seconds and in a course of nearly seven hundred yards, ten seconds is not very long.

However, 'zero points' came the announcement over the loudspeakers and at once there was deafening applause for a very popular rider, so much so in fact, that it was almost impossible to hear the announcement that followed. 'Correction, correction.' A pause. Suddenly there was a tense hush in the stadium and one could imagine the anxiety of d'Inzeo, although he continued walking Fahnenkonig out of that great Aachen arena, apparently placidly.

'Correction.' Everybody was tense, waiting. 'Raimondo d'Inzeo, Italy, on Fahnenkonig, time faults: $1\frac{1}{4}$ time faults.'

Needless to say, this announcement was made in German, and so, if one did not understand German – and I for one did not – it was impossible to know how many time faults d'Inzeo had had. The announcement was repeated in French, and now I was confident that I heard the score correctly. Finally it was repeated in English, and so the time faults were confirmed as $1\frac{1}{4}$; this meant, of course, that d'Inzeo finished up with $1\frac{3}{4}$ faults, whereas Goyoaga had finished with three, thus giving him a margin of $1\frac{1}{4}$ faults.

It was certainly a most interesting and dramatic competition, and one which was almost certain to start fairly heated discussions all over the world. Who wants to allow other riders to ride their best horses? This was the argument. Nevertheless, one feels bound to say that it does put the premium on the rider, which surely is right in a riders' world championship. It is not a world championship for horses: that, of course, is left to the individual event of the Olympic Games.

Certainly there could be no worthier world champion than Raimondo d'Inzeo. It was particularly apt that the holder of the previous World Championship, Hans Winkler, should present the award, the more especially as he was still suffering from the injury he received when jumping that second remarkable round on the great German mare, Halla, at

Stockholm in the Olympics, suffering appalling pain. It was incidentally, the second occasion on which d'Inzeo had won the World Championship.

Since 1956 this has been the way in which the World Championship is competed and since then I have been lucky enough to see a number of very exciting competitions. How well I remember, for instance, the first time that David Broome reached the final of the World Championship. He was, of course, riding that brilliant Sunsalve – a horse which proved quite beyond most of the other riders. In fact, it did not pave the way for a Broome victory; nevertheless, it did result in the most crashing fall for the American Bill Steinkraus at the water jump – the water would appear to be Steinkraus's unlucky fence.

Obviously a competition such as this is open to a certain amount of gamesmanship, and people take – sometimes – a perverse pleasure in jumping a horse that they know will be extremely difficult for the others to ride in the final. It would not be entirely unfair to say that David Broome's World Championship success at Hickstead in 1970 was due to the fact that Beethoven was not an easy horse to ride.

In that particular World Championship at La Baule the four finalists were David Broome with Beethoven, Graziano Mancinelli with Fidux, Harvey Smith with Mattie Brown and Alwin Schockemöhle with Donald Rex. So, for the first time, one nation had two riders in the final. David Broome went clear with his own Beethoven, Mattie Brown and Fidux – a notoriously difficult horse to ride – but had one rather careless error on Donald Rex. His total, therefore, was four. Mancinelli was clear on his own Fidux, clear on Donald Rex, but he had 4 faults on the two British horses and it cannot, I think, be denied that his riding of them was very erratic. Harvey Smith had an unexpected stop on Mattie Brown and 2 time faults; he had time faults again on Donald Rex, though only threequarters of a fault. On Fidux and Beethoven he had 4 faults each : total $13\frac{3}{4}$. Schockemöhle, without any doubt David Broome's greatest rival had a clear round on his own Donald Rex, but he seemed unable to steady Beethoven at the water, where he had 4 faults, as he did on Fidux and then Mattie Brown went somewhat ungenerously for him and so he collected 8 faults for a total of 16.

It was interesting that Donald Rex had only one fence down in the whole competition – and that was when he was ridden by the new World Champion, David Broome. Fidux proved a problem for all the riders except Mancinelli, but what was so impressive was the calm way in which David Broome handled him, coaxing a very much more attractive round out of him than for his own Italian rider. In the opinion of Harvey Smith, Donald Rex is the best horse that he has ever ridden, though of course he only rode him for a matter of minutes. Neither is it without interest that Shockemöhle, who probably started favourite and certainly started favourite for the European Championships, some eight years earlier, was robbed of victory by faults at the water. At the White City in 1962, his nearest rival was David Barker riding Franco, and he seemed all set to win the World Championship when, in very bad going, he took a really crashing fall at the water.

At the Courvoisier Championships at Wembley in the autumn of 1972, David Broome confirmed his position as World Champion, for at this meeting the week after the Horse of the Year Show, a world-style event was staged. This was known as the Courvoisier Cognac Champion Horseman and it was fought out between the four highest placed riders from qualifiers in two previous competitions. David Broome had earned two final placings, but he was only allowed to ride one and he chose his Olympic mount Manhattan rather than Ballywillwill, who was, in fact, the leading qualifier. The next best qualifier was the young Irish rider, twenty-two-year-old Eddie Macken, on Iris Kellett's Easter Parade – Iris Kellett was one of the earliest winners of the

Queen Elizabeth Cup and, except for a period of illness, has remained at the top of the tree for over twenty years. The other British finalist was Ted Edgar, who of course is David Broome's brother-in-law – and it is interesting that at one time or another both have had Discutido, the 1956 World Championship finalist, in their stable. In this event Ted was riding Everest H.I. The fourth finalist was the young German rider, twenty-two-year-old Hendrik Snoek on the Hanoverian-bred, Shirokko, who pipped Raimondo d'Inzeo and Ann Moore by just one point for the final.

It was an eight-fence course, ending with a big double, but in the first round, it was only Ted Edgar who had a fence down; this was the wall at number six. In the second round, Broome went clear on Everest H.I. and Easter Parade notched up a clear round for Snoek, but Ted Edgar found himself a little out of control on Shirokko and had the first part of the double down, while Macken on Manhattan had the second part down. This meant that Broome and Snoek were equal with a zero score at the end of the second round, while Macken was third with 4 faults and Edgar fourth with 8 faults.

The final round was exciting in the extreme. Easter Parade dragged a pole off the second fence when ridden by David Broome. This took David's total to 4 and it meant that Snoek, if he went clear, would win the competition. He was riding Everest H.I. and was going really well until suddenly he found himself confronted with a little problem of steering – for which later he was to blame himself, incidentally – and had 8 faults. So it was David Broome who once again was the winner of this world championship type of event, and a very deserving winner he was, for each horse that he rode – even Shirokko, who must probably be one of the most difficult horses in the world to ride – had gone really well for him.

Hendrik Snoek was a worthy runner-up, showing great ability with strange mounts in this very small and confined arena : a very different kettle of fish to riding a strange horse in a big ring. Had it not been for his one mistake with H.I. there would inevitably have been a jump-off – and it is worth remembering that Shirokko, only a few weeks earlier, had won the Hickstead Derby. Obviously it is impossible to say who would have won, but I would be surprised if the majority of the audience and those watching on television had not plumped for the German horse.

This very promising young Irish horse, Easter Parade, was the most successful of the horses incurring only 4 faults, but Everest H.I., which in fact is a German-bred horse and was only a novice at the start of the season, was the horse that most of the riders seemed to think was the easiest horse to ride, other than their own. Certainly this is an interesting kind of competition, though whether it can really claim effectively to find out the leading rider must be open to a certain amount of doubt for the simple reason that, as I have suggested, riders are not likely to put in their very best horse which could so easily become unsettled by the methods of a strange rider. From the public's point of view this sort of competition is, of course, a winner, and therefore I shall be surprised if it does not continue to have a place in show jumping, particularly in the World Championships.

From a personal point of view, I always associate that first four-horses-four-riders World Championship in Aachen in 1956 with a somewhat odd experience. I had been sent out to cover the final, which according to my briefing was due to start at 6 o'clock. I, therefore, arrived via plane to Dusseldorf and train to Aachen at about 5 o'clock only to find the whole competition in its final stages. It had started at 4 o'clock – or 16.00 hours. Unfortunately someone at the B.B.C. had wrongly translated 16.00 hours into 6 o'clock!

The viewing public, therefore, were denied a competition of great interest of which I alone, at some cost to the B.B.C., had been privileged to enjoy.

Chapter VIII: *Amazons*

Over the years there has, not surprisingly, been quite a considerable amount of controversy connected with show jumping. Obviously, the more popular and the more publicised a sport becomes, the greater the pressures; and so one can expect more controversy. In the early days controversy was something almost unheard of, so I remember well the surprise at the controversy that arose out of an event at the Horse of the Year Show when it was still held at Harringay.

It was 1955, and the event was the *Sunday Graphic* Cup; this is the Victor Ludorum, now known as the Ronson Trophy. As now, it was a two-round competition, and at the end of the second round only two riders had achieved double clear rounds. These were Pat Smythe and Dawn Palethorpe.

For some years Pat had been the unrivalled lady champion. It is no exaggeration to say that she was the darling of the show jumping world; she could do no wrong. Her horses – first, Finality, then Tosca and Prince Hal – were household words, and the fact that she had bought each of these horses for a sum of money which, in show jumping today, would be considered derisory, endeared her to the public the more. She had got where she had by her own skill, her own effort and her own dedication.

There then appears on the scene Dawn Palethorpe. Her sister, Jill, had already shown that riding was in the family's blood, for she herself had won the Queen Elizabeth Cup at the White City in 1950 on Silver Cloud. But in the eyes of the public Dawn had privileges which were denied to Pat, coming as she did from a wealthy Worcestershire family.

As far as the show jumpers themselves were concerned

55

there could be no more likeable or more dedicated rider than Dawn. She had taught herself; the horses that she rode were, when first produced by her, no more the proven article than Tosca and Prince Hal had been when first Pat rode them. In particular, she had an Irish-bred mare called Earlsrath Rambler and, although this horse stood well under 16 h.h. it quickly proved that it was capable of jumping very big fences. More than that, thanks to the skill with which Dawn had trained it, and the way in which she rode it, they were capable of executing turns which used to have the crowd gasping and so, again and again, she proved herself capable of winning a big event against the clock.

In 1955 she was well-known as a formidable competitor, but it was Pat Smythe who was still very much at the top of the tree, and in the opinion of the ever-increasing number of show jumping followers, the leading lady in the world of show jumping.

As is usually the case with two experts, Pat and Dawn had a healthy respect for each other, but there was certainly no animosity; probably it would be true to say that the existence of the one put the other on her mettle, and so the rivalry between the two was very keen – especially with the Olympic Games looming ahead less than twelve months from the Horse of the Year Show : the first Olympic Games in which lady riders were to be allowed to compete.

In this final for the *Sunday Graphic* Cup, Pat had to go first. She was riding Prince Hal. She went clear, as she had already over the course twice, and she clocked the astonishingly fast time of thirty and one-fifth seconds. This time seemed to the crowd a winning time, for Pat was so experienced and Prince Hal so fast and so handy, that surely the comparatively inexperienced Dawn Palethorpe and Earlsrath Rambler could not possibly beat it.

In fact, she did. Her time was thirty seconds dead; she had won by one-fifth of a second. The gasp, which had a very easily recognisable note of anger in it when I announced the official time, was one of my less happy memories as show jumping commentator. The crowd had nothing against Dawn Palethorpe, but they wanted Pat Smythe to win. She had been beaten by one-fifth of a second, which, in their opinion, was not a measurable difference.

What was one-fifth of a second? A dilated nostril? The nose of a horse breaking the timing beam, rather than its chest? How could one horse possibly be considered the winner when there was so little difference in time?

This seems strange to us today, when we now go down to one-tenth of a second, even in show jumping. In other sports they can go to one two-thousandth of a second, as happened in the swimming in the 1972 Olympic Games. In 1955, however, this accurate timing was something quite new; the spectators had not got used to it, just as they were only beginning at that time to accept the racing photo-finish, whereby one horse can be adjudged the winner of many thousands of pounds at the expense of another, by almost literally a whisker.

The buzz of grumbling went on as Dawn Palethorpe left the arena; the applause that she received when she returned for the awards was very moderate compared with that which was accorded to Pat Smythe.

Surprisingly, the next day the papers took it up, and this started a stream of correspondence – both public, in the newspapers, and privately to the B.B.C., or to myself. The gist of the grumble, which to me seemed unreasonable and really quite ludicrous, was that Dawn had had the advantage of wealth, background, privilege, was able to purchase expensive horses and so on, whereas Pat had had no such advantages. The majority of writers seemed to think that it should have been a tie but, as I patiently pointed out, in any sport a result is better than a tie; furthermore, that under international rules a result was considered essential. Finally I drew the grumblers' attention to the fact that, only a few weeks earlier, Pat herself had won a major competition by a fifth of a second. There had been no complaints then. Oddly enough, in the same event just a year earlier, it was Pat who had beaten Dawn, though not by quite such a small margin.

As for the privileges and opportunities, this was sheer nonsense, for both Pat and Dawn had got to the top by hard work, ability and determination – three qualities that are absolutely indispensable in any athlete wishing to reach the top and which nothing else can replace.

No one had worked harder or had been more conscientious in her approach to show jumping than young Dawn Palethorpe. An example of this was in Rotterdam, 1956, just a year after she had pipped Pat on the post at the Horse of the Year Show. Since then she had not been quite so successful; she had found herself all too frequently standing in second place – as often as not below Pat. She had failed to make the Olympic team for Stockholm. She decided that it was now time that she won, and won something big.

The Grand Prix in Rotterdam was the event she had set her mind on. That morning she rose at the crack of dawn and put in long hours of work on Earlsrath Rambler to make sure that he was at his very peak of suppleness that afternoon.

In the first round fourteen went clear; both Pat and Dawn were included. The final jump-off was over a very big course in very difficult going, and it was of course against the clock. Pat unfortunately had a fence down. Raimondo d'Inzeo, on Uruguay – the horse on which his brother, Piero, whose mount Uruguay usually was, had won the King George V Gold Cup a few weeks earlier – went clear in forty and two-fifths seconds. He then went clear on his usual mount, the brilliant Merano, in thirty-eight and four-fifths seconds. This latter round seemed unbeatable, so fast, so accurate, so quick on the cornering was it, but when Dawn came in she seemed to know instinctively that she could beat it. And beat it she did; riding with breath-taking skill and a dash unknown even to her, she clipped one-fifth of a second

off d'Inzeo's time. So acute was her turn through the treble
that her left leg actually grazed the upright as the horse
landed and made for the wall that followed it. Raimondo
said afterwards that it was an honour to stand second to a
performance such as Dawn's.

Earlsrath Rambler was an astonishingly versatile horse.
He could jump at speed; he could jump the big fences; he
could win at Puissance – as, in fact he did at Aachen. Dawn
used to ride in a very individual style, with rather a loose
rein, almost as if she were throwing her reins at the horse
to get the best out of it. She seldom checked, a fact which
makes it interesting to contemplate, how, were she to come
back now, her style would compare with the style of riding
today, when there does seem to be a good deal more checking
than in the days when Dawn was at her best.

I want to conclude this chapter on a rather happier note
than the *Sunday Graphic* duel between Pat Smythe and
Dawn Palethorpe, which produced such unfortunate controversy. It was at the Horse of the Year Show in 1964.
That year happened to be the centenary of the death of the
great Robert Smith Surtees, the creator of Jorrocks. It was
decided, therefore, to produce a display at the Horse of the
Year Show entitled 'Jorrocks Rides Again'.

In this display, which I had the honour of devising and
producing, there was depicted many of the most famous
Surtees characters, the parts being played by leading personalities of the horse world. What a cast list!

John Jorrocks	George Hobbs
Pomponius Ego	Ronnie Marmont
Richard Bragg	David Barker
Mr Puffington	Douglas Bunn
Lord Scamperdale	John Lanni
Jack Spraggon	Derek Kent
Soapey Sponge	Fred Welch
Facey Romford	Alan Oliver
Lord Ladythorne	Sam Marsh

Miss de Glancy	Jennie Bullen
	(now Loriston Clarke
Lady Scatterdash	Cynthia Haydon
Mrs Barrington	Christine Mossman
Miserimus Doleful	Jane McHugh
Belinda	Iris Gates
James Pigg	Harry Goddard
Mr Fleeceall	Raymond Brooks-Ward

It is worth noting that Sam Marsh, who only died in 1972 had taken part in the famous displays in the early days of Olympia. But it was, of course, Jorrocks who stole the show. George Hobbs was ideally cast, and night after night his appearance with James Pigg and the hounds would bring the house down. He looked exactly as the Leach drawings depicted him – fat, jovial, earthily common – and night after night the crowd rose to him. It was altogether a delightful display and, for many people who had attended the Horse of the Year Show regularly for anything up to twenty years it is one of the richest memories of that great show.

In the Victor Ludorum on the final night George Hobbs was a competitor and, to the intense delight of the crowd, who had just been revelling in his Jorrocks in the Surtees display, he pulled off a dramatic and an exciting victory, which absolutely brought the house down.

George, now Chairman of the B.S.J.A. Rules Committee, is – and has for a long time been – one of the most popular show jumpers in the country. He never changes; it is not often that he has hit the headlines. He has not perhaps had as many major wins as he deserves – was he not second four times in the King George V Gold Cup? George Hobbs and others of his sort are the very backbone of show jumping. They are the riders who can be depended upon never to let a side down when they represent their country, can be relied upon regularly to bring on good, new horses with international potential which, in all probability, they cannot afford not to sell when they have got them near the top. These are the stalwarts of show jumping. More exciting or dramatic meteors may flash across the heavens and, for a year or two, thrill the public with their exploits, their successes or simply by their personalities; but it is such as George Hobbs who keep show jumping going, not only at the international level but at the less glamorous but vitally important level of the county show, the one-day show or the two-day show, which rely on people of this calibre both to ensure that there will be good jumping and to attract a good gate.

Show jumping owes much to the Second XI – even if they are not very often associated with the most memorable moments of show jumping or those events which really hit the headlines. They surely are the grist which keeps the mill turning.

Chapter IX *Triumph and Disaster in Mexico*

I have always thought that, for sheer drama, it was the Mexico Olympics that had the most of all; and I have been fortunate enough to be involved directly or indirectly with all the Olympic Games since 1948. Helsinki, of course, was a tremendous thrill because of the British team winning the gold medal at the very last minute, after Foxhunter's débacle in the first round; but for the ups and downs of fortune surely there has been nothing quite to equal Mexico.

To begin with, there had been a good deal of acrimonious controversy over the selection of our show jumping team. David Broome and Mister Softee were obvious choices. For many people no team could be complete without Harvey Smith – whether he had an Olympic horse to ride or not. The Maverick, ridden by Alison Dawes (at that time she was Alison Westwood) had probably the best record of any international horse, but people always insisted that this great horse had a stop in it. Then there was Marion Mould (at that time she was Marion Coakes) and her little pony Stroller. Stroller was only 14.2 h.h.; how on earth, people asked, could a pony like this be expected to jump an Olympic course?

Nevertheless it was Stroller who joined Mister Softee, Harvey's Madison Time and The Maverick as our final Olympic squad.

There are two show jumping events in the Olympic Games – the individual and the team event. It is up to the local Olympic Committee that is running the Games to decide whether they have two separate events or whether they jump the individual as part of the team event; as in fact they did in London, Helsinki, Stockholm and Tokyo, whereas in

Rome, Mexico and Munich, they jumped as two separate events. In the individual event, if it is run separately, each country was only allowed to enter two horses, but since Munich the number has been increased to three. This always creates a problem because, unlike any normal show, when the most important event comes at the end after the horses and riders have had several days of 'warming-up' experience, at the Olympics a rider goes straight in the deep end. The one chance a rider has of getting Olympic experience for himself and his horse is if he can ride in the individual event before the team event – the team event always being considered the more important.

But with only two allowed to jump in the individual, it meant that one rider, until Munich, had had no chance of the vital warm-up. Inevitably, therefore, there was a certain bitterness amongst those who were left out of the individual competition. In Rome it proved disastrous for Britain, as the young Franco and David Barker were left out of the individual and unfortunately had three refusals in the team event, which put Britain right out of it.

In Mexico, the selectors decided to jump Stroller in the individual. Most people, I think, assumed that the policy lying behind this was, as it were, to get Stroller out of the way as this pony could not seriously be considered for a place in the team. Stroller and Marion Mould would have their chance; it was confidently anticipated that they would not disgrace themselves, but most people were quite sure that the form they would show in the individual would never justify their being selected as one of the three in the team.

The other to jump in the individual was Mister Softee with David Broome riding. Their selection was obvious because not only had this combination won the European Championship, but David Broome was already an Olympic bronze medallist. It meant, however, that two horses who would presumably be in the team four days later – The Maverick and Madison Time – (though there was still some doubt as to which horse Harvey should ride – O'Malley or Madison Time) would enter the team event with absolutely no previous Olympic experience of any sort.

In fact, things turned out quite unexpectedly. The course was a big one and was jumped in two rounds. The first was a typical Nations' Cup course – some fourteen or fifteen fences, all of them big but fair. The second course was a puissance-type course and held an enormous set of parallels – one of the biggest fences that has ever been built. It was the first course, however, that caused an unexpected amount of trouble, for although it seemed fairly straightforward, horses were making mistakes regularly, though not always at the same fences. The first to go clear was the American rider, Bill Steinkraus on his Snowbound. This was a really good horse, though there had been doubts about its complete soundness. However, Bill Steinkraus had no less than four Olympic Games behind him and, as the American team captain, was one of the most experienced riders at the Mexico Olympic Games. A number of horses had 4 faults, including Mister Softee, and the only other to go clear as the first round neared the end was the diminutive Stroller. This superb round by a gallant little pony and a wonderfully skilled and courageous young rider, brought the huge crowd to its feet and hopes were certainly high within the English camp.

In the second round, over the really big fences, it was these great parallels that caused all the trouble, only one horse, out of all those still in the event, managing to jump it – a number of horses had bad falls. Even Snowbound was unable to clear it, Mister Softee just failed to make it and Stroller quite obviously disliked it, as, in an effort to make the spread, he had to do an awkward twist which brought his hind legs down on the final pole, which then rattled between his legs nearly bringing him down himself. Unable to get properly balanced before the last fence, he then had this down as well, which meant that Steinkraus and Snowbound ran out as clear winners of the gold medal, with Marion and Stroller safely holding on to the silver.

For the bronze there would have to be a jump-off, as there had been in Tokyo in 1964, when once again a British rider was involved. But whereas in Tokyo it was the veteran rider Peter Robeson (who had been reserve to the Olympic team in Helsinki in 1962 and a member of the bronze medal team in Stockholm in 1956) jumping against the comparatively inexperienced John Fahey of Australia, in Mexico David Broome had four against whom he had to compete. He had the advantage, however, of going last and he made the most of his luck of the draw. Knowing exactly what he had to beat, he went round that great, though now shortened course, with his usual flair, and notched up his second Olympic bronze medal.

After this the selectors' task was even more difficult; how could they possibly leave out a horse that had won a silver medal? Especially in view of the fact that the team course was expected, as usual, to be slightly less demanding than the individual course. If Stroller were included, then who should be left out? Harvey Smith? It was surely unthinkable, though many felt that his good young horse, Madison Time, was hardly ready for the Olympics. It was rumoured, too, that Harvey himself would have preferred to ride O'Malley, but the selectors had doubts about O'Malley's complete soundness.

If Harvey was included then it meant leaving out Alison Dawes and The Maverick – perhaps the most experienced combination in international jumping at that time. No one, however, can blame the selectors for deciding that Mister Softee and Stroller really selected themselves and that Harvey Smith, even though his horse was less experienced, was of such inestimable value to any team because of his tremendous experience, his professional approach to the sport and that famous will to win, that he could not be ignored.

So, finally, the British team consisted of Harvey Smith on

C

Madison Time, Marion Mould on Stroller and David Broome on Mister Softee, and that was the order in which they jumped.

The course was open to inspection at 7 o'clock in the morning, the competition due to start at 8 o'clock. In fact, the start was put back until 9 o'clock, so there was plenty of time for everybody to walk the course and inspect it really thoroughly. During the hour or so in which I was looking round the course myself I encountered riders and trainers from practically every nation taking part. I heard no one complain that the course was too big; the general comment was that just as at Munich, four years later, it was big but fair.

However, when only two or three horses had gone, it became quite obvious that the course was riding far bigger than one had anticipated and indeed far bigger than the course-builder had intended. The reason for this was that the turf in the centre of the great Olympic stadium had never had a single horse's hoof on it until the first horse jumped on that final day – the individual event having been held in a different stadium. There had been a lot of rain in Mexico during the Olympics, and beautifully green as the turf looked in the main stadium, it was in fact, superficial turf that had been put down especially for the Games. In consequence there was none of the spring that one expects to find from natural turf and, because of all the rain, the shallow turf that covered the arena had become gooey. The result of this was that the horses were getting no help from the turf at all; not only was it dead but it was definitely holding. This meant that every fence was jumping a few inches higher, and in spread fences, a few inches wider, than the measurements suggested. Therefore a fence was perfectly fair by the official measurements, but in practice it became on occasions so big as to be almost unjumpable.

As usual it was the combinations that caused the most trouble; the first was a treble with a high wall of 5 ft. 3 in., and then two sets of wide parallel poles as the second and third elements. The problem here was that if a horse jumped accurately enough, and high enough to clear the wall, then it found that it had not the impulsion to reach the two sets of parallels; so horse after horse was 'ballooning' over the wall and then either stopping at the first or second set of parallels or crashing through them.

The second combination was a double of rustic poles and these were true parallels; in other words, each pole was exactly the same height as the others, the sort of fence that is always regarded as the most difficult fence of all, for even if one pole is only an inch lower than the one beyond it, it is easier for a horse to jump. To add to the difficulties of this particular double, it had been placed only some eight or nine strides from a 16 ft. water jump, so that it was extremely difficult for a horse that had been really extended to get over the water, approaching it at full gallop, to steady back quickly enough to be able to jump the double accurately – and exceptional accuracy was demanded.

In the first round none of the British team cleared the treble; both Madison Time and Stroller jumped the wall but could not make the parallels. Mister Softee hit the wall and managed to get through the parallels. Mister Softee did the fastest time, though this was really of no importance except the time allowance being so strict many horses collected time faults. Nevertheless, at the end of the first round, with many horses collecting what can only be described as cricket scores, Britain and Canada were way ahead, so that it really did look as though Britain would win another medal.

As a rule, horses jump better in the second round because they know the fences and their riders know the problems. For instance, it was Harvey Smith who had realised that the best way to attack the treble was to sail on at the wall, chance taking a brick out (which would admittedly cost 4 faults), but at least then one would still have the impulsion to clear the two sets of parallels; whereas to 'balloon' over the wall and then make a mess of the parallels could easily result in one's picking up 3 faults for a refusal as well as a fence down.

Admittedly, because of the heat horses jumped less well in the second round at Helsinki: it is also true to say that, because of the size of the Olympic course, horses do tend to tire and it is possible, therefore, that they will jump a little less well in the second round. In Mexico, however, one did somehow feel confident that our horses and riders, with their great experience, would have benefited from the first round when they could appreciate to the full exactly what the problems were.

For Britain, Harvey Smith was the first to go and, although he put into practice his new theory about the treble, he still collected 12 faults, but other horses going first for their respective countries did no better. In fact, Harvey's was the best score after the first horse from each country had jumped. We still had our better horses, Stroller and Mister Softee, to come.

Then, of course, disaster hit us. Stroller, in fact, was not enjoying the Olympics. There is little doubt that that huge set of parallels in the individual event, when he found that he was literally physically incapable of jumping it, had upset him. I believe that if Stroller had been involved in a jump-off in that individual event, then almost certainly he would have made it quite clear to the spectators – and particularly to the selectors – that he had had enough of Olympic fences. He would then not have been asked to jump again in the team. But he was not involved in a jump-off and so he finished with a silver medal, and, as I have said, his selection was obvious; he could not possibly be left out.

But Marion Mould knew very well as she rode him in, even before the first round, that he was not really himself. It has been suggested that his tooth was giving him trouble although the veterinary surgeon had insisted that he was 100% fit to jump. My own conviction is that he remembered the course of four days earlier. If he had been in

68

something of a state before the first round, he was in an even worse state before the second when he now knew what those great combinations were like. Jumping the practice fences, which were some way away from the main stadium, he certainly was not inspiring; so much so that David Broome remarked to his father as they came down to the stadium that he thought Stroller might easily be eliminated. Certainly the pony entered the stadium sweating badly. This, of course, must have been extremely unnerving for poor young Marion.

The memory of the next few minutes is still something of a nightmare. Stroller, reaching the treble, jumped the wall without fault, but just could not make the first of the parallels. He stopped. There was a gasp from the stadium and a great hush as Marion took Stroller round to try again. Again they cleared the wall, but this time he slipped into the second element – the first set of parallels – and collapsed with the poles flying all round him and his unhappy rider. One of these hit Marion in the face and dazed her; she was quickly on her feet, but Stroller lay there – he was unable to rise. For a terrible moment it seemed as though he had broken his leg, a thought which obviously flashed through Marion's distressed and hazy mind. In fact, he was only lying on his rein, which prevented him from getting up. An official quickly released him and, with great relief, Marion re-mounted. They started rebuilding the fence but Marion, still suffering from a mild concussion, and remembering perhaps the refusal she had in the first round at the double, somehow imagined that she had been eliminated, although she had had only two refusals. Accordingly she started to ride from the arena. As she approached the exit, Harvey Smith came rushing down and yelled at her; he was trying to make her realise that she could still go on, but for a moment the penny did not drop – or, perhaps, in the state in which she was in, she did not clearly hear Harvey.

Eventually she realised what the situation was and cantered Stroller back to jump the great treble yet again. Somehow – and this courageous effort of both Stroller and Marion seems to have been forgotten when people remember the Mexico incident – on this third occasion they got through the treble, but they had the poles down. A great cheer went up, a cheer of relief after the agony of the last few moments, and away Marion went to jump the last few fences of the course. Then, as she jumped the fences across the middle, suddenly the bell went and we realised with horror that, because of that delay after her fall and because Marion had forgotten to signal to the judges that she was ready to start again as soon as the fence had been rebuilt, she had run out of time. She had exceeded the time limit; it was not just a case of exceeding the time allowance when faults would be added for overtime, she had completely exceeded the time limit, which is double the time allowance.

This could mean only one thing, that Britain, having been at the top after the first round, was now right out of it because, by the rule, in the case of an elimination the horse that is eliminated takes the worst score of the whole competition and then adds twenty extra faults.

The irony of it is that even after that disaster, had Marion got round the course, Britain almost certainly would have won a medal, so high were the scores of most teams; but it was not to be, and what had started with such a triumph when the gallant little pony had won a silver medal in the individual event, finished with such a disaster when the huge parallels had proved beyond the physical ability of this pony.

For the record, Mister Softee and David Broome did another good round, but it was too late to relieve our fortunes, and it was Canada that ran out unexpected but worthy winners of the team gold medal at the Mexico Olympic Games.

Chapter X: *Misfortunes in Munich*

There are many reasons why the Olympic Games at Munich will go down in history as one of the most sensational of all the Games since first they were resurrected in 1912. Tragically, the occurrence that will be chiefly remembered is the disaster which befell the Israel athletes, but many of the other events were dramatic in themselves, and though the Games were flavoured by this tragedy on the second Tuesday, one hopes that many exciting and worthwhile results will also be recalled when the Games have become history.

The equestrian events, as usual, provided a great deal of excitement – not only for those who were riding enthusiasts, but for many others some of whom were seeing show jumping for the first time in their lives and even more were experiencing for the first time the thrill of a Three-Day Event.

For the British Three-Day Event team it was triumph all the way; after a more-than-passable effort in the dressage phase, the British riders excelled on the second day across country, Richard Meade in particular riding a brilliant round on Major Derek Allhusen's Lauriston to score the best marks in that phase. On the third day, in the show jumping, the brilliant way our riders tackled the twisty course gave them an outstanding victory, beating their nearest rivals, the Americans, by no less than a margin of eight fences.

This was a great start to our equestrian hopes. The fact that in the Grand Prix de Dressage, Mrs Lorna Johnstone on El Farucco was the first British rider ever to reach the 'ride-off' in Olympic Dressage was also heartening, especially in view of the fact that many considered she had been harshly marked. The judges all the time seemed to prefer the more solid type of dressage as practised by the Germans, whereas Mrs Johnstone had adopted the French style which, in the opinion of many, is more pleasant to watch, though admittedly less accurate.

After these two encouraging events great hopes were held for the show jumping.

As in Mexico the individual event and the team event were held separately – the former being held in the magnificent new stadium which was the centre-piece of the remarkable equestrian complex at Reim, while the team event was held as usual on the last day of the Games in the main Olympic stadium.

The British team consisted of David Broome, Harvey Smith, Ann Moore and Michael Saywell. The first two, of course, had competed at Mexico. Ann Moore, the reigning Ladies' European Champion, a previous European Junior Champion and a member of the British squad for the Ladies' World Championship held in 1970, was an almost automatic choice, as her form throughout the season had been marvellously consistent, particularly on Psalm. The surprise choice, therefore, was Mike Saywell, though his horse Hideaway was a real Olympic-type horse and had jumped very generously and successfully throughout the season. There were many who thought that Paddy McMahon and Pennwood Forge Mill should have been included – and a few weeks later, after the Horse of the Year Show, were even more sure that he should have been included; but that is a story to be told a little later on. It was indeed unfortunate that The Maverick, ridden again by Alison Dawes, should have to withdraw shortly before the Games because of unsoundness. Other possibles were Peter Robeson – a veteran of the Olympics since 1952 – and Raymond Howe with his spectacular Australian-bred grey, Kalkallo Prince.

It was, in fact, Peter Robeson who was once again the reserve, as he had been no less then twenty years earlier, having meanwhile won two Olympic bronze medals at Stockholm in 1956 and in Tokyo in 1964.

Early in the season many people assumed that Ann Moore would ride the Australian-bred April Love if she made the Olympic Games, as this horse had already jumped in the Olympics, representing Australia in Mexico in 1968. For this reason April Love was given a very easy time during the first three or four months of the season, Ann Moore confining herself to Psalm for the big events, and to novice horses for the less important events. However, when April Love was brought out, she immediately had trouble. For some weeks she was not at all well and eventually it became quite obvious that, if Ann was to make the Olympic team, it would be with Psalm.

I, for one, was not sorry, because I had not been particularly impressed with April Love's performance in Mexico, whereas every time I saw Psalm jump it seemed to me that here was a horse that would give his all. Ann Moore herself is also one who will stop at nothing; she is not only a brilliant horsewoman, but she has a wonderful temperament and is no less determined than her horse. Indeed, there is no doubt that it is her own determination that communicates itself to her horses.

There were, however, those who suggested that Psalm could not be relied on to jump a really big combination, but the selectors preferred to believe the evidence of their own eyes, having seen Psalm jump many combinations as big as any that he was likely to encounter in the Olympic Games.

Psalm and Ann Moore were one of the three chosen by the selectors to jump in the individual event at Reim. There were some who were of the opinion that she had been chosen simply to give her experience that would be of value when it came to the team event a week later. There were others who genuinely believed that she had it in her to win a medal, but these, I am inclined to believe, were very much in the minority – perhaps the wise-after-the-event brigade! After

73

all, she would be jumping against the very best in the world, and not only lady riders – indeed, there were only two other lady riders in the whole event – but the leading male riders, including the d'Inzeos, the great German riders, Winkler, Steenken; the Americans, Steinkraus and the rest of his team and, indeed, many others who had all at one time or another won Grands Prix in the very best international company.

Nevertheless, it was Ann alone of the British squad, which consisted of David Broome, Mike Saywell and herself, who was involved in the jump-off. As usual, the course consisted of two rounds, the first course being severe enough but the second course not only being considerably bigger, as it was in Mexico, but much longer than it was in Mexico, consisting of twelve really big fences, including a double and a treble.

It was, in fact, the double that robbed Ann of her first chance of winning the gold medal – a point not generally appreciated. The double followed a set of high white poles, 5 ft. 3 in. high, a very upright fence demanding great accuracy. Immediately acceleration was necessary if one was to have sufficient impulsion to clear the wide rustic poles that formed the first part of the double and then be able to reach the second element.

Psalm met the upright perfectly but he jumped so big that he slightly dislodged Ann, so that she lost her left stirrup. The double was only some eight strides away and Ann hesitated for a split second while she found her stirrup, knowing only two well that, if she attempted to jump this huge fence – quite the biggest on the course – without a stirrup, it could only spell disaster because of Psalm's very erratic style of jumping. She could easily fall off altogether or, because she was not riding properly, allow Psalm to become unbalanced at either the first or second element.

But that moment's hesitaiton meant that Psalm just lost his impulsion and so had both elements of the double down.

74

Having gone clear over the first course this meant that he had a total of 8 for the two courses, thus tying with Mancinelli of Italy and Nial Shapiro of America. Had she not lost that vital impulsion she would almost certainly have got away with only one part of the double coming down and thus she would have finished with only 4 faults and been the outright winner of the gold medal, with no need to jump-off at all, as was the case with Steinkraus in Mexico.

But these things happen: indeed, this is what competitive show jumping is all about. Nevertheless, her two brilliant rounds on Psalm had assured her of a bronze medal, but could she perhaps go one better? It was still more than a possibility, especially with having the advantage of going last.

The American, Shapiro, went first and, in a time that was by no means unbeatable, had two fences down for 8 faults. Then it was Mancinelli's turn. Riding like a man possessed, on a horse that had been bred in Ireland and had not been spectacularly successful since being ridden on the continent by Mancinelli, he nevertheless managed to get round this great course clear, but again in a time that did not seem to be unbeatable.

The crucial point in his round – and it was ultimately to prove the decisive moment of the whole individual event – was between the second and third fences from the end. The penultimate fence was a very big treble; Mancinelli jumped the fence before it and then, deciding that the shortest way to get to the treble was to turn sharp right-handed, go back on his tracks and then turn in the shape of the letter 'S' left-handed again into the treble. This meant two checks and, being wise after the event, I doubt whether in fact he saved time by turning to the right after the third last instead, as others had, of turning to the left and swinging round on a left-handed sweep to come back to the treble.

Ann Moore – or possibly her father, who is her trainer and adviser – realised that an 'S' turn such as this was out of the question for a horse like Psalm, and so they decided that they must find somewhere else where they could save a precious second.

It seems that Ann Moore, realising how brilliantly Psalm was jumping, decided that it would be possible to cut a corner between the first fence, which in the jump-off was a very big triple bar, and the second fence which was a high, upright poles – now raised to 5 ft. 5 in. She therefore came in very sharp and there is little doubt that Psalm did not realise until too late that he was expected to jump a fence. People sitting in the stands by the fence said that as he came round the corner he was looking straight at them in the stands, not aware of the fact that he was expected to jump the fence on his right.

Ann wasted no time turning him round, taking him back and jumping the fence at the second attempt, but it was 3 faults for a refusal. She then sailed round the rest of the course perfectly, not attempting the 'S' manoeuvre between the third and second last, but sweeping round on a left-hand rein. Naturally her time was slower than Mancinelli's because she had had this refusal which necessitated a turn and going back several yards, so that she could have a proper run at the second fence. In any case, she had 3 faults, but having watched the film several times and used a stop watch on it, I have little doubt that her time, had she not stopped, would have been faster than Mancinelli's. It would appear – although it is impossible to be wholly accurate in a case like this – that the time she took to stop, turn and go again at the second fence was just over two-fifths of a second longer than the difference between her time and Mancinelli's. In other words, had she gone clear, she could have beaten Mancinelli by just over two-fifths of a second, and so would have won the gold medal.

Thus, in the space of half an hour, Ann Moore had had the experience of an Olympic gold medal twice slipping through her fingers but, wonderful sportswoman that she is, she made not the slightest complaint, merely admitting that she had made an error of judgement in the jump-off in trying to cut too tight a corner between the first and the second, and insisting that she was as thrilled as she possibly could be at winning a silver medal in the Olympic Games.

And indeed she might well be, for she was only the second lady rider to win an individual medal in Olympic show jumping.

Obviously, as with Marion Mould and Stroller in Mexico, it was unthinkable that Ann Moore and Psalm should be left out of the British team for the team jumping the following week, the others in the team being David Broome on Manhattan, Harvey Smith on Summertime, and Mike Saywell on Hideaway.

Few people really believed that anyone could beat the German team, though their showing in the individual event had been extremely disappointing. Nevertheless, it was quite obvious that they had benefited by their experience in that event.

High hopes, however, were entertained for Britain, especially when Hideaway, going second in the team, collected only 8 faults at the end of the course. This was considered a very promising start. Harvey Smith on Summertime going first had gone well, but could have gone better. All went well with Ann Moore and Psalm until they came to the treble towards the end of the course. This was a really big fence and the distances were demanding: certainly it had caused more trouble than all the other fences put together. It seemed as though Psalm had not quite got the right stride as he approached the fence, hesitated, hit the first two parts, then failed to reach the third part and dodged out. Ann quickly took him back and, with great courage, rode through successfully on the second occasion, meeting the fence absolutely right, which was obviously of paramount importance.

David Broome's round on Manhattan was quite outstanding, as somehow he coaxed this far-from-easy horse round with only one fence down, for 4 faults.

77

At the end of the first round, therefore, Britain was in a strong position, though Germany had a healthy lead. The actual scores at the end of the first round were as follows:

Germany	–	16
U.S.A.	–	$16\frac{1}{4}$
Great Britain	–	23
Spain	–	23
Italy	–	32

In the second round the weather had improved, it having been very cold for the first round. Yet, strangely, the horses did not jump so well. An exception was Summertime, for Harvey Smith. Using all his familiar guile and determination, Harvey somehow got his horse round with only one fence down, and that was a careless brick out of the wall. Hideaway seemed to be going really well but, at the end of the course, had precisely the same two fences down as he had in the first round, suggesting perhaps that this great horse may be lacking a little in stamina when it comes to really long, demanding courses.

Britain still looked in a very strong position when Ann Moore came in on Psalm. She jumped all the first part of the course fluently and brilliantly but, when it came to that great treble, there was trouble once again. This time she met it wrong, hit the second part and ran out at the third. Back she went only to do precisely the same.

Ann obviously was upset, and it is indicative of her great character, her real professionalism and her personal courage, that she unhesitatingly tackled this great treble yet again, knowing that the faults that she had collected there almost certainly could rob Britain of a medal. Psalm's courage was no less than his rider's and they jumped perfectly at the third attempt, cleared the last two fences and earned the great cheer they received as they left the arena – for Ann Moore had certainly become the darling of the Munich crowd.

It was strange how history seemed to have repeated itself.

In Mexico, Marion Mould had had trouble at the big double in the individual event yet had nevertheless won the silver medal, and then, in the team event, had had a disaster at the treble which had put paid to Britain's chances. Now, in Munich, Ann had had trouble in the individual event double yet had still won the silver medal and then, in the team event, had had a disastrous experience at the treble.

But now, thanks to the team consisting of four riders, with only the best three to count as in an ordinary Nations' Cup – whereas in Mexico and all previous Olympics the team consisted of three riders all of whom had to count – there was still a chance for Britain because David Broome and Manhattan were still to come, and in the first round, they had only 4 faults.

But the unbelievable happened; two mistakes early on gave David 8 faults but, when he jumped that huge treble clear and there were only two fences to go it seemed certain that Britain must win a bronze medal.

Unbelievably, he hit the second last and then it was obvious that Manhattan was back in one of his awkward moods and was really paying no attention and making very little effort. It was as though he had suddenly got bored with the whole thing and, despite the tremendous efforts of David Broome to get him going properly and really to concentrate on the job and to jump the last fence with the ease with which he had jumped it in the first round, Manhattan met it wrong, rather screwed over it and carelessly knocked it down. So Britain was just pipped for the bronze medal – a heartbreaking experience for the whole team, not least David Broome, who had done everything a rider could do to get his horse to jump those last two fences well enough to clinch the medal.

Obviously this was very disappointing for Britain, but the Olympic Games has a history that is full of drama such as this, of the ups and downs of fortune, of the unexpected and even of the tragic.

Germany, as expected, were the winners, but only just, for here again there was drama of a high order.

In the first round only Steinkraus had done a clear round; if he could go clear again in the second round – and he was the last to jump for the United States, then America could beat Germany. The horse was jumping as superbly as ever but, when it reached the water, it seemed not to take off at all and just galloped through it. This, of course, cost him 4 faults and the team gold medal. Just what happened is impossible to tell, because in the first round the horse had jumped the water perfectly, though it is true to say that he made something of a mistake at it in the individual event. Bill Steinkraus was riding in his sixth Olympics and although he himself won an individual gold medal in Mexico, it would have been a fitting end to his great international career to have led the United States team to a team gold medal.

The courses at Munich were probably the best courses ever built for Olympic show jumping; they were designed by Brinckmann – undoubtedly the best course builder in the world. The result was that, although the courses were big, they produced excellent results and jumping of a very high order. In the individual event the worst score of all was in the thirties, whereas in Mexico there were scores round about the hundred mark. In the team event, where obviously with the less good nations you are going to get some bad horses included, there were some worse scores, but there were no disasters and very few horses were eliminated.

For this reason I am inclined to think that the Munich Olympic Games, from the equestrian point of view, were the best of any since 1948, when they were held in London. It would, indeed, be tragic if show jumping were dropped from the Olympic Games, for surely no more fitting spectacle than the show jumping, coming immediately before the closing ceremony, could be devised. One has to admit, too, that show jumping holding this place of honour has a great

LEADING LADIES
Above: Dawn Palethorpe, heroine of the fifties, on Earlsrath Rambler. *Below:* Ann Moore, heroine of the early seventies, on Psalm.

MOMENTS OF MISERY IN MEXICO: Marion Mould, and Stroller, winner of the Individual Silver Medal, in one of the most dramatic incidents ever in an Olympics. Stroller, failing at the second attempt to make the second element in the treble, slips.

Stroller's hind legs slide under him—

—causing him to fall backwards.

Stroller, cast, is held down until Marion releases him.

Marion is helped back into the saddle—

—and the 14.2.h.h. Stroller flies over the 5ft high 7ft wide treble at the third attempt.

'THE GOOD OLD DAYS'—BEFORE THERE WAS MONEY IN IT!
Above: Olympia 1926: Morning session: elegant harness.
Below: Olympia 1929: Gala matinée: parade of prize winners.

opportunity to arouse an interest in the sport amongst many people who have previously never had any knowledge of the sport.

From Britain's point of view Ann Moore was, without doubt, the heroine of the equestrian Games. This young girl enormously enhanced her reputation, and by her performance she has done what Pat Smythe and Marion Mould did before her; that is, been an inspiration to many young riders who feel that they would like to aspire to the heights reached by these great lady riders, all of whom have got their by their own skill and whole-hearted dedication.

Chapter XI: *New Blood*

It is always exciting when a new name hits the headlines. So often the Horse of the Year Show, in the early days at Harringay and since 1959 at Wembley, has been the occasion on which a new name has come to the fore. Only a few years ago it was Graham Fletcher who suddenly, from a comparatively unknown background, won major competitions and the prize for the leading rider of the Show at the Horse of the Year Show. Then, in 1972, there was the dramatic appearance of Pennwood Forge Mill.

In fact this great young horse was no newcomer. Indeed, there were many who believed that he should have been chosen for the 1972 Olympic team – thanks both to his ideal Olympic conformation and the consistency of his jumping. In fairness to the selectors, however, it should be made clear that his most impressive jumping came after the team had been announced. This was probably due to the fact that Paddy McMahon, having established a wonderfully successful partnership with this horse, was desperately keen to get into the Olympic team, and as is so often the way when a rider is overkeen, he started pressing.

From the ringside, and watching it on television, one got the impression that he was riding the horse right to the bottom of every fence so that it got as close as possible before take-off. This tended to give the impression that the horse lacked scope; in fact, there is little doubt that it was simply a case of over-anxiety with his talented young rider.

Once the team had been announced and there was no longer any possibility of Paddy McMahon and Pennwood Forge Mill being included, then Paddy relaxed and immediately this combination hit winning form. It is almost true to say that from then until the end of the season they swept the board. Certainly they finished up having won more prize money than any other horse registered with the B.S.J.A.

Without doubt, however, it was the last night of the Horse of the Year Show that finally clinched their success, and made them public heroes.

The Horse of the Year Show in 1972 was remarkable for the strength of the international opposition. This was due to two things. First, the Olympic Games had been held in Germany only a fortnight earlier; secondly, the Horse of the Year Show was to be followed immediately by the Courvoisier Championships – a new event staged at Wembley and sponsored to the tune of £20,000 by the famous brandy firm. Not surprisingly the foreign riders were dominated by the Germans, three of their four Olympic riders being involved, and certainly they showed very strong form; indeed, at the beginning of the week, it looked as though they were going to be unbeatable.

Two riders, however, held them at bay in two of the most dramatic show jumping events I can ever remember. The first was the Puissance in which Ray Howe on the Australian-bred horse, Kalkallo Prince was the only horse to jump the wall at 7 ft. 3 in. The great German horse, Der Lord, ridden by Hartwig Steenken, and Pennwood Forge Mill, ridden by Paddy McMahon, narrowly failing. The latter, in fact, jumped the wall best of all with a perfect take-off and cadence, describing the perfect parabola which is necessary in a really good jump, showing indeed the immaculate bascule that Caprilli himself was so keen on, but he just tipped the coping off the top of the wall.

Der Lord did not hit it hard but the coping on the top of the wall moved across, overbalanced and fell. Kalkallo Prince, however, with a great high jump record in Australia, seemed to meet it completely wrong, got right underneath it and appeared to have no chance whatever. However, he screwed over it and although he hit it hard with his hind legs, the wall stayed put. Few who were there or who watched it on television will forget the ecstatic way in which Ray Howe threw his hat into the very roof of Wembley as he recovered from the jump and galloped out of the arena.

This great performance had certainly won the admiration of the vast crowd; Germany at last was being held at bay. But it was on the last night of all that the crowd really rose to a British victory. In the final event – a two-round competition for the Victor Ludorum of the whole show – there were eventually four British riders, three German riders and young Eddie Macken from Ireland, showing such remarkable promise in his first international show, left in with a chance. These were the riders who, out of twenty-five starters, had achieved double clear rounds.

Simona, ridden by Steenken for Germany, went first and had a clear round. From then onwards, over this very demanding course being jumped against the clock, there were no clear rounds until the third German rider, Paul Schockemöhle (the brother of the more famous Alwin) riding Abadir, came in and managed to beat Steenken's time by a full two seconds. This really did seem to be absolutely invincible.

Pennwood Forge Mill entered the arena. This horse stands well over 16 h.h., but so deep is he through the girth, so short and strong are his legs, that he gives the impression of being a small stocky horse rather than a big one. Paddy McMahon looked anxious as he rode him round waiting for the bell, and it seemed as though the crowd, too, were anxious to show their appreciation of the fact that Britain was still in with a chance. Defeat seemed probable, yet many in the audience who had either been there in person or had watched it on television had not forgotten Forge Mill's great performance in the Puissance two nights earlier, or his magnificent effort in the Hickstead Jumping Derby when he may well have been unlucky not to have won, or the effortless way in which he dominated the Olympic trial at British Timken. But surely, against the clock, in a small indoor arena, this was not Forge Mill's metier at all.

Yet, somehow, that vast, tense crowd sensed that Paddy McMahon and Forge Mill were determined to win. I have never heard on any other occasion a cheer start as a horse approached the first fence. It was as though the moment the bell had gone and the last British horse had started the pent-up emotions had been released. It was as though the crowd hoped that Forge Mill could be borne on the wings of a cheer – and so it was. As he rose at the first fence, the cheer started. It increased in a steady crescendo as he went round the course of eight fences. As he turned for the last two and the crowd somehow found themselves able to snatch a glance at the great electric clock hanging over the centre of the arena, they realised that Forge Mill could, in fact, beat Abadir's time, and so this tremendous cheer rose now to a vast shout – of ecstasy, excitement, hope and anticipation.

Unbelievably it all worked. I do indeed believe that Forge Mill and Paddy McMahon were inspired by that tremendous cheer, finding somehow a reserve of strength previously un-known to them and, more important, a reserve of speed. As Pennwood Forge Mill flashed through the finish the clock stopped and then ten thousand pairs of eyes turned to it. Twenty-eight point three; Forge Mill had won the Ronson Trophy from the might of Germany by just .1 of a second.

It was not the rider this time who threw his cap into the air as he left the ring; rather it was the spectators, who threw anything and everything that they could lay hands on in the air. Seldom, if ever, have I witnessed such a scene of rejoicing.

Certainly Pennwood Forge Mill and Paddy McMahon were the heroes of the hour, and they returned to a tre-mendous reception when they came in to receive the trophy; a reception repeated a few minutes later when they took their place in the great cavalcade that brings the Horse of the Year Show to an end.

Even at the time of the Olympic Games it was being rumoured that the owner of Pennwood Forge Mill, Mr Hartill, had refused £50,000 for the horse. Later it was claimed that the offer had been stepped up to £60,000. By November it had been announced that Mr Hartill had made it quite clear that he would not accept £100,000 for this great young horse.

This, of course, is generosity of a very high order, for obviously no horse, even with the increased prize money, is going to win anything like £100,000 – or even £50,000 – in the whole of his career. The value, therefore, is one of prestige and there is no doubt that those from overseas who are offering such vast sums for horses of this calibre are doing so because they want their team, their nation, to achieve international success, just as Mr Hartill obviously hopes that Forge Mill will be included in the 1976 Olympics, jumping for Britain – and not against Britain.

The Horse of the Year Show, being followed immediately by the Courvoisier Championships, inevitably meant that the latter could be assured of jumping of a very high standard, for most of the riders who had jumped at the Horse of the Year Show naturally were anxious to stay and compete for the big money being offered by Courvoisier. The leading event on this occasion was the final championship for the first prize of £3,000, the biggest prize ever offered for show jumping. It is worthy of mention in this chapter, because it brought to the fore another young rider of whom there is no doubt much will be heard during the next few years.

His name is Derek Ricketts, who comes from north Buckinghamshire, where his father has for some years run a successful, but quite humble, coal business. Derek learned his riding on a pony, on the Qainton Hills, frequently with the Bicester Pony Club, and hunting regularly with the Bicester and Whaddon Chase hunts.

He first came to the notice of the experts riding a horse called Beau Supreme, but just as he had brought this horse patiently, but quite quickly and very successfully to the top, an offer was received for it from Belgium, which made it almost inevitable that Derek Ricketts would lose it, and so it turned out. However, he was fortunate in that Mr and Mrs Cox, enthusiastic horse lovers, decided to buy a show jumper and, being involved in the travel business, they called it Tyrolean Holiday. Wasting very little time, Derek Ricketts brought this good horse, which used to be called Garnet, to the top. As Garnet, its success had been considerable, but certainly not spectacular. And then, on the last night of the Courvoisier Championships, Derek Ricketts was to make it very nearly immortal.

There were six clear rounds at the first jump-off, four of which came from Germany – Robin, Torphy, Simona and The Robber. Ann Moore on Psalm and Derek Ricketts on Tyrolean Holiday were still in for Britain. In the first jump-off Ann Moore hit the planks, as did The Robber, so in the final jump-off against the clock it was three of the four German gold medallists from Munich, and young Derick Ricketts. Fritz Ligges, on Robin, came in first, but he had two elements of the treble down in a time of 32.7 seconds. Hans Winkler, with four gold medals under his belt, was clear on Torphy until the very last fence – the planks, which he just touched and they toppled, in 36.8 seconds. Then in came Simona, ridden by Steenken, and this great mare with her brilliant young German rider, made it all look so easy; not only did they go round the course effortlessly, clear, but they went in a remarkably fast time – 30.1 seconds. It seemed, therefore, as the comparatively inexperienced Tyrolean Holiday came in, that there was going to be a clean sweep for Germany.

And yet, so easily, Derek Ricketts might have achieved what Paddy McMahon had achieved a week earlier. Disastrously he just rapped the very first fence carelessly – a set of crossed poles, after which he completed an absolutely faultless round. Having had the first fence down, and knowing therefore that he could not win, he did not really turn the taps on, taking the sort of risks that he might have done – and might well have got away with, as is so often the case when a horse is jumping a course that it has jumped before – yet his time was only one-fifth of a second slower than Simona's time. In other words, had he not carelessly rapped that first fence, he might well have pressed on realising that great £3,000 first prize was within his grasp, and finished with a faster time than Steenken, instead of a fractionally slower time.

Nevertheless, the performance had won him and his horse the admiration of the crowd – in addition to the second prize of £2,000. Ricketts and Tyrolean Holiday had refused to capitulate to the might of Germany and by their heroic challenge had provided yet another great moment in international show jumping.

Testimony to Derek's ability has been underlined by the fact that despite the big figure at which Beau Supreme changed hands, his new owner, having failed to make his mark, returned him to Derek who has immediately taken him back to the top.

Chapter XII: *A Notorious Gesture*

There is no doubt one of the most sensational incidents in show jumping history occurred at the Hickstead Derby in 1971. This was the occasion on which Harvey Smith, riding Mattie Brown, won the Derby for the second successive year – the only horse ever to do so – but it was only after months of wrangling, stewards' inquiries and recriminations, to say nothing of fantastic Press coverage, that Harvey was finally allowed to keep the £2,000 first prize.

Oddly enough it was I who, indirectly and quite unconsciously, was at any rate partially responsible for the whole incident. On the Friday of the summer meeting there was a competition which concluded with a jump-off against the clock. Harvey Smith, riding Johnnie Walker, was amongst those who qualified for the jump-off and, in fact, was drawn to go last. When he came in John Kidd was in the lead with a fairly fast time. This competition was being televised and, when Harvey Smith approached the end of his round, I noticed that the clock, which was also visible to viewers in the corner of the screen, stopped just before he actually took off for the last fence.

As the finish was some fifteen yards the other side of the last fence, it was quite obvious that Harvey Smith's time should have been at least two or three seconds longer than actually was announced, for the judges, naturally, took the time from the official timekeepers' apparatus, being unaware of the fact that, by a mischance – a human error consisting of a sudden unfortunate nudge of the timing box – the clock had stopped early, and so awarded the first prize to Harvey Smith and Johnnie Walker.

But in my commentary, quite involuntarily, I alluded to the fact that the clock had stopped and, therefore, Harvey Smith had not really completed the round in the time that the clock showed. I did not labour the point but, with millions of television viewers, even during an afternoon session, it was not surprising that a large number picked up what I had said and, realising that Harvey Smith should not have been awarded the competition, telephoned in to the show or to the B.B.C. to say that there had been a mistake.

Naturally, their complaints came to the ears of the judges; more important, they were also reported to Mrs Kidd, John's mother, the owner of the horse which would otherwise have won the competition.

Many people felt that, in view of the fact that she is a wealthy woman, and herself a director of Hickstead, she should have let the matter pass. On the other hand, wealth is really beside the point when it comes to sport and just as the owner or the trainer of a horse belonging to a millionaire will object if, in a race, their horse for one reason or another has been prevented from winning, so it was really quite understandable and justifiable that Mrs Kidd should object when, from all that she had heard, it was quite obvious that her horse, ridden by John, should have won.

The only concrete evidence, of course, was the television; fortunately – or possibly unfortunately – this particular competition had been recorded on video-tape and so when the judges asked if they could see it, it was quite obvious that the producer was in a position to show them the film, even if he were doubtful as to the wisdom of doing so. I personally was strongly opposed to it for the simple reason that I felt it was creating a dangerous precedent when, in any sport, it is possible for a player or competitor to appeal to the evidence of a television camera. One can imagine all too easily the chaos there could be if every referee's decision to disallow a goal because a player was offside was questioned, a final decision being made depending entirely on the television coverage of the incident.

However, after considerable pressure had been brought to bear, the producer agreed to show the judges the film. Not surprisingly as soon as they had seen it, they realised that the competition had been wrongly awarded to Harvey Smith and that it should have been John Kidd who won, as his time must have been at least two seconds faster than Harvey Smith's. Accordingly, the decision was reversed and Harvey Smith and Johnnie Walker were placed lower, the event being awarded to John Kidd.

This made a difference of some £40 as far as the prize money was concerned. Not for one moment did anybody imagine that Harvey Smith was seriously worried at losing £40, nor could they have imagined for one moment that Mrs Kidd objected in order to increase her winnings by £40 : it was simply a matter of principle. However, I cannot help feeling that it was in a somewhat cavalier manner that the result of the inquiry was made public – a notice simply posted on the board saying that the result had been altered. Harvey Smith had not even had the opportunity to attend the showing of the film; had he been, and if the judges had said to him, as almost certainly they would have done, 'You must see for yourself that this is a false result; don't you think it would be better if you yourself asked for the result to be altered?', I have little doubt myself that he would have agreed, and there would have been no bad feeling. But Harvey Smith can, at times, be a somewhat prickly customer and there is no doubt that he was offended by the way he had been treated, being quite unprepared to consider the rights and the wrongs of the situation. He preferred to suggest to those who would listen that quite wrongly the judges had decided the competition on the television time rather than on the correct time; in fact, the television time was merely a reflection of the correct time.

For some time relations between Hickstead and Harvey

Smith had been a little strained; this, therefore, was just an additional item to sour even further the relationship between the two strong personalities, Douglas Bunn and Harvey Smith. Mrs Kidd, being a fellow director of Hickstead with Douglas Bunn was, therefore, in Harvey's eyes, very much under the Hickstead bracket. To make matters worse, the human error responsible for the mistake was attributable to Mrs Bates-Oldham, another Hickstead director, who for many years has been responsible for the department which takes care of the timing apparatus.

So, when it came to the great Derby itself, Harvey already felt that he had a grievance. The Derby consists of two rounds, the second round for those in the lead with an equal number of faults, and of course, against the clock. In all the Derby's history there have been very few clear rounds and, on this occasion, there was no clear round. In the first round, only Stephen Hadley riding Prospero and Harvey Smith riding Mattie Brown had 4 faults. Prospero refused at the poles at the bottom of the bank, and a single time fault to bring his 3 faults for a refusal to a total of 4; thus it could be said that he was unlucky not to have won outright for, had it not been for the time fault, he would have had 3 faults to Harvey Smith's 4. In the second round, against the clock, but over a much shorter course – which did not incidentally include the famous bank – Prospero had three fences down which made it appear that the prize had more or less been handed to Harvey on a plate.

That, however, was not the case, for Mattie Brown had been one of the last to jump in the first round and coming in for the second round, was obviously still fairly exhausted. (The Hickstead Derby course is the longest course in show jumping.)

He had a pole down at the second fence; he then had the first of the double white gates down, which meant that he had to jump the rest of the course clear. Naturally there was considerable tension, chiefly because Harvey Smith is always an extraordinarily popular competitor with the crowd and on this occasion was in with a chance of becoming the first rider ever to win the famous Hickstead Derby two years running. But there was also a few who knew something of the tension behind the scenes.

With plenty of time in hand, Harvey jumped the last few fences carefully and accurately, and so he won the Hickstead Derby for the second year running, with a margin of 4 faults, or one fence down. Not surprisingly he was highly delighted. One cannot, in my opinion, blame him for letting his excitement, his relief, his triumph, run away with him, especially in view of the fact that he had been going through a fairly lean period prior to the Hickstead meeting. As he passed the directors' box he made his famous gesture which brought forth a big laugh from all those close enough to see it. He, of course, insisted that it was V-for-Victory sign. My own impression is that, whichever the sign was – and one has to admit that it is not easy to see from the frame of the television film of the incident whether the sign was one way or the other – he was, in effect, saying, 'Now what about your £40? As far as I am concerned you can keep it because I have just won £2,000, so sucks to you' – or words to that effect!

It is significant that in Harvey Smith's own book *V is for Victory**, he maintains that those in the directors' box had made it quite clear that they hoped he would not win; secondly, that he made his sign 'on my right hand in the direction of that balcony over-looking the Devil's Dyke; it was a V-for-Victory; it was meant to show how delighted I was that Mattie Brown had become the only horse ever to win the British Jumping Derby in successive years.'

I have to admit that I personally saw no evidence of the mockery of which apparently Harvey was conscious emanating from the directors' box. But more important, it must be pointed out that the balcony was not overlooking the

* Published by William Kimber & Co. Ltd.

Devil's Dyke, which was right down the opposite side of
the course, whereas the directors' box was up on the top side
of the course, almost immediately opposite the finish and
adjacent to the members' stand. Admittedly, since this particular incident, the directors' box has been moved to a
position overlooking the Devil's Dyke and immediately above
the B.B.C. commentary box, but in 1971 it was at the top
of the arena. If Harvey Smith says, as he does in his book,
that he made the sign in the direction of Devil's Dyke, then
inevitably it suggests a certain confusion in his recollections
of the whole incident.

It is, in all probability, as well known as any story connected with show jumping, how Harvey Smith heard, driving
through the night on his way home to Bingley in Yorkshire,
that a telegram had been despatched to him, informing him
that he had forfeited the prize 'for disgusting behaviour'.
Nevertheless, it is worth, I think, considering briefly the
whole affair and its implications from a more detached point
of view.

I myself heard the announcement about the telegram
driving home from Hickstead, and have to admit that I was
appalled at the way that the situation had been handled,
whatever the rights and wrongs of the incident may have
been. Next morning, I attempted to telephone Douglas Bunn,
but was unable to contact him. I wrote, however, saying that
I felt that the way the matter had been handled had done
a grave disservice, both to Hickstead and to show jumping.
I urged him to make an immediate announcement to the
effect that he and his fellow directors had acted precipitously
and had since decided that the right thing to do was to
refer the whole matter to the stewards of the B.S.J.A. I
appreciated that this would be something very difficult to
do and would demand great courage, but I was absolutely
convinced that, for the sake of Hickstead and show jumping
generally, to say nothing of Douglas Bunn's name and reputation, this was the right thing to do.

On receipt of my letter Douglas telephoned me and told me how greatly he appreciated my writing, but that he felt nevertheless, after consultation with people whose opinion he trusted absolutely, that his original decision should be adhered to. I told him that naturally I accepted this, as it was in any case nothing whatever to do with me, but that I still felt that what I had said was right and further, that I believed that I was acting in his own best interests to have written as I had done.

To my great relief, twenty-four hours later, it was announced that there was to be a stewards' inquiry : meanwhile, the decision and the prize money were to be held in abeyance.

For one reason or another the inquiry itself was not the most creditable part of the B.S.J.A.'s history – in fact, at times it came near to being a farce. At the first inquiry the television film failed to turn up, as insufficient time had been allowed for the vagaries of the post; it was, therefore, hardly of value for the stewards to listen to various witnesses putting their side of the story. On the resumption of the inquiry the film was produced, but opinions seemed divided as to exactly which way the famous sign was intended. Naturally, the stewards gave Harvey Smith the benefit of the doubt and in due course he received the first prize of £2,000.

This famous gesture of Harvey Smith's at Hickstead in July 1971 has obviously endeared Harvey to the British public, has made him a personality of the same ilk as Fred Trueman, Gordon Pirie, George Best and other famous figures in sport, who appear to be 'agin the Government' and anti the Establishment; in fact, once all the publicity is swept away, one generally finds that such people are simply independent characters, dedicated to their sport, people who nevertheless are not prepared to toe the line just because they are expected to or because other people do so. (It is not without interest that so many of these strongly independent, self-willed characters seem to come from the north of England!)

It is said that no publicity is bad publicity, that a person or a sport will always benefit ultimately through the publicity it or he or she receives, even if the publicity is of a kind that does not appear to be very flattering. Certainly the publicity that Harvey's gesture produced made him a household name – in his own words, his attendance, subsequent to the Hickstead incident, at a show could double the gate – and it is possible that it has made more people interested in show jumping, by increasingly turning the spot light on the sport; yet I cannot help feeling that there is a reverse side to the coin. I believe that all the publicity and the incident itself did tarnish slightly the image of show jumping as a happy, respectable, genuine sport; but more than that, I believe it created a false picture of Harvey. I have little doubt in my own mind that Harvey would like to be able to attribute the fact that he is the most famous name in show jumping the world over to the winning of a gold medal at the Olympic Games in Munich or Mexico, rather than to the raising of two fingers at Hickstead in 1971. I fear that famous gesture might possibly have falsified Harvey's own position, he may feel that because he is a world famous name, the sport is more dependent upon him than it really is; hence his turning professional and all the ballyhoo that has accompanied his decision.

Yet he must know, better than anyone, that to maintain his position and his reputation, it is absolutely essential for him to have top class horses on which he can consistently *win*. Without success, the ballyhoo surrounding him will quickly prove to be ephemeral. He must stay at the top: it is vital for his image.

It would be very sad if the Harvey bubble were pricked for he is without doubt not only one of the greatest show jumping riders that the world has known in the last twenty-five years, but he is – and this is even more important – a real competitor. Every time he rides into an arena he rides in to win. As he has said himself : 'I am not interested in being second.' He can coax performances out of indifferent horses in a way that nobody else can. It would indeed be sad to see him slide from the top simply because he found himself unable to live up to the reputation that he had, almost fortuitously, come by.

One has seen all too often, in many different sports, the performance of an athlete going down as the pressures become greater; there is no doubt that the pressure on Harvey Smith is going to be very great indeed. It might even be true to say that the fact that he has, since Hickstead 1971, had a comparatively lean time is attributable to the immense pressures to which he has been subjected ever since that unforgettable incident at the end of the Hickstead Derby?

One can but hope that he will rise above it all and prove once again that, in addition to being a great character of the kind which will always appeal to the crowds, he is also a great competitor and an outstandingly brilliant horseman, whose fame rests entirely on his skill as a rider and trainer of jumpers and not on a cheap gimmick.

His new mount, Hideaway, which I suggested in public Trevor Banks should let him ride in the Olympics at Munich, might well be the answer.

Chapter XIII: *A Dream Comes True*

1945 – and one of the greatest moments in show jumping; only four months after VE-Day. This may sound incredible, but it is true, and because it was such a memorable occasion the future of show jumping was assured.

The story really starts back in 1940, when hundreds and thousands of young soldiers, officers and men, were taken prisoner-of-war and carted back into Germany to spend the rest of the war in prisoner-of-war camps. In one camp, to relieve the boredom, it became the custom for each member in turn to give a talk on any subject of his choice. In May 1942, one of the young prisoners-of-war decided to give a talk on show jumping; the idea aroused no great enthusiasm. Indeed, to quote the speaker himself, 'When the groans had died down, I assured them that it would not be as dull as it sounded.' He intended, firstly, to give the talk as though it were a running commentary on some show jumping event of the future. Secondly, he was going to use an assistant, who would demonstrate certain things and also draw diagrams, etc., on – not a blackboard because they had no such thing – but on a piece of old newspaper with a bit of charcoal. These two – and they were known as the Long and the Short of it, as the speaker was very tall and the assistant was very short – made the talk so interesting that, in this prisoner-of-war camp they formed a riding club.

They did, obviously, lack one rather essential commodity, a horse : but they did very well with an upturned tea chest, a saddle made out of papier maché, bits of string for the reins, pieces of wire for stirrups and so on and, although it was obviously impossible to do any practical riding, this did not really matter as the object of the club was to carry out a research into jumping : something that had not been done before. People took it for granted that horses could jump because they had seen them out hunting, or in the local point-to-point, or the Grand National on film, but in fact a horse is not a natural jumper such as a cat or a fox, but can only jump in the same way as an aeroplane takes off. In other words, it needs the weight and the speed of its approach down the runway to make it airborne. It is the same with a horse : it can only jump if its momentum is increasing, which is why one talks about 'maintaining impulsion'.

As, in this prison camp, there were a number of famous cavalry regiments represented it was not surprising that there were many people who had spent a lifetime with horses in one way or another. There were jockeys, men who had worked in racing stables, in studs, in riding schools, in hunt service; people who had learnt just about all there was to know about riding and the behaviour of horses, and so, between them, they amassed a great deal of knowledge.

This knowledge was co-ordinated into a kind of thesis on jumping. In its way it was quite revolutionary, but little can those prisoners-of-war in 1942 have ever imagined that their research in wartime Germany would result in a step forward in show jumping that was of greater importance than anything that had so far occurred in the history of that sport.

At the end of the war, when the prisoners were re-patriated, they could not wait, understandably, to put their theories into practice and some went round to the offices of the British Show Jumping Association, only to find that they were closed, for the Association had become virtually mori-bund. However, they dug out the Secretary from his retire-ment in the west country and they asked him to call a meeting. This meeting was held in June 1945 in London, and some thirty-five people attended it. The first item to do was to select a chairman and, by only a narrow margin –

99

in fact, one vote – the 'Long One' was elected, much to the dismay of many people who knew little of his ability. His immediate reaction was certainly surprising. He went down to the end of the room, locked the door and put the key in his pocket. Returning to the Chairman's table, he then explained that the object of the meeting was to put show jumping on the map and that, to do this, it was necessary to start with something that would really cach the imagination of the public, including the Press. This must be a competition with a bigger prize than had ever been competed for before; that prize must be not less than £100. Therefore, he was going to ask everybody to empty their pockets and get out their cheque books until between them they had collected £100; he would then unlock the door!

In fact, £108 was collected which meant they were able to announce a new show jumping event to be called the Victory Championship, with a first prize of £100, a second prize of £5 and a third prize of £3!

The next problem was to find somewhere to hold the event, for most open spaces in wartime England had been requisitioned. Fortunately, however, they were introduced to a certain Mr Frank Gentle, who was then the Chairman of the Greyhound Racing Association. So impressed was he by their enthusiasm that he generously suggested that they should hold the competition at the White City. For twenty-four hours it was to be theirs to do what they liked with and all his staff would be at their disposal. This was a very generous gesture which was to pay handsome dividends.

It is not difficult to imagine the excitement with which the course was designed and constructed along the lines of all the theorising that had taken place in the prisoner-of-war camp. Eventually the fences constructed at Aldershot were brought up to London and erected in the White City Stadium. By 5.30 p.m. on the evening before the competition the course was complete and those who had qualified for the event – about twenty-four – were invited to inspect the course.

By six o'clock all but one of the competitors had withdrawn his entry, having decided that the course was quite impossible. Instead of the simple course in a figure-of-eight consisting for the most part of gorse hurdles and simple poles, here was a course of sixteen or seventeen fences in doubles and trebles, facing in all directions and, far from being simple hurdles and poles, the fences were in gay colours and, where there were gaps, they were plugged with flowering shrubs or pot plants or oil drums painted in gaudy colours : even the water jump was dyed sky blue. Worst of all, the high white wings which used to stop the horses running out had been removed, and in their place were narrow uprights with flags flying at the top. As one of the competitors said, all this undoubtedly looked very picturesque from the stands, but the horses would have nothing to do with it.

So an impasse had been reached, with the much publicised great Victory Championship less than twenty-four hours away. However, by ten o'clock, thanks to the persuasive powers of the Chairman and, in all probability, the consumption of a considerable amount of alcohol, all but one of the competitors had decided to have a crack at the course next day.

Next day was Saturday, September 1st, 1945; without doubt one of the most important dates in the whole history of show jumping. It was just exactly six years since Hitler had marched into Poland and just as that September 1st in 1939 had been the beginning of the end for so many millions of people all over the world, so September 1st, 1945 could be described as a new beginning for show jumping, a sport that was to catch the imagination of millions.

What happened that afternoon was to have tremendous repercussions. The first real excitement came from the fact that, out of the twenty-three starters, seventeen jumped clear rounds; this was because they were for the first time jumping a course of fences that had been, as one might put it, scientifically designed. The distances between the fences had been carefully worked out and measured. The fact that a horse jumps better if there is a bold ground line had been produced in the building of the courses. The fences were inviting – at the same time they were formidable, forcing a horse to concentrate fully.

In those days there was no jump-off against the clock – rather there was a succession of jump-offs until the judges decided they'd had enough. On this occasion there were no less than five rounds, but in the end there were only two riders left. One was that great horseman and show jumper, Ted Williams, who at that time was at the very top of the tree, but who was to have another twenty-five years in international jumping. Not only was he in a leading position with his great horse, Umbo, which had been the outstanding horse during the war-time jumping in Britain, but he also had two other horses, Huntsman and Leicester Lad, well in with a chance. The other rider was none other than the 'Short One' – Colonel Nat Kindersley, who had returned from his prisoner-of-war camp to find, to his delight, that his old favourite, Maguire, had been bought for the sum of £40 by his wife when all army horses were sold with the mechanization of the cavalry in the early days of the war. The horse was no longer young – over eighteen, in fact – but he had always been a good jumper and had frequently represented the army before the war.

In the final jump-off it was Ted Williams who had to go first, and he collected just half a fault. In those days it was the custom to lay a narrow slat across the top of the poles which could be displaced at the cost of half a fault, without the whole fence being knocked down, the emphasis being at that time in b.s.j.a. jumping, very much on accuracy. The slat did not, however, last very long for the wind was always blowing them off – or at any rate the riders were saying that it was the wind that had blown them off, and not their horses which had knocked them down. Consequently, there was endless controversy and nobody was really sorry to see them disappear.

When Nat Kindersley on Maguire came in, however, it was a clear round to win. The fences were now very high, having been raised for each jump-off, but the old horse and his skilled and experienced rider (though he had been out of the saddle for more than five years) jumped as well as ever until they came to the very last fence.

This was a high, white upright gate and because it had been frequently raised there was now a gap of nearly eighteen inches between the bottom bar and the ground; this lack of ground line made it an extremely difficult fence and it was probably for this reason that Maguire stopped almost dead.

At once a groan went up from the audience, many of whom knew the story behind the inclusion of Colonel Kindersley and his old Army charger in this final of the Victory Championship. It was almost as though Maguire heard this groan, for suddenly he launched himself into the air: not like an aeroplane but rather like a helicopter! Somehow he screwed over that gate; he hit it with his forelegs, he hit it with his hindlegs, but when he landed just about on all four legs, almost facing the gate such a screw had he made as he jumped it, the gate was swinging and shaking and rattling, but it did not fall down.

Something that had been no more than a dream within the grey walls of a prisoner-of-war camp in Germany had now become a reality in the famous White City Stadium in London; a fairy-tale ending if ever there was one and, for those present, one of the most memorable moments in show jumping.

Fairy-tales, however, tend to have a sad element, and this one was no exception, for the one person who would never personally be able to enjoy the new style of show jumping that he had inspired was the 'Long One'. He, of course, was

Colonel (now Sir Michael) Ansell, but what Mike Ansell lacked in physical sight he more than made up for with his mental vision. He was determined that show jumping was a sport at which the British could succeed; he was determined that, with drive, energy, perseverance, show jumping could well and truly be put on the map as a great national sport.

How right he was to be proved, but he would be the first to admit that he was, in those early days, aided and abetted by one or two people present that afternoon. In particular, there was Mr Frank Gentle of the G.R.A., who had been so impressed with the Victory Championship that he generously suggested that the International Horse Show should be revived at the White City rather than at Olympia, where it had been held before the war; and, were his offer accepted, he undertook that the G.R.A. would stand all the show's losses for the first three years and share any profits equally. This generous gesture made it possible to revive the International Horse Show in 1947 at the White City (it only became the *Royal* International Horse Show ten years later, on the fiftieth anniversary of the first International Horse Show held at Olympia in 1907).

Colonel Harry Llewellyn was another who was impressed by the Victory Championship; so much so that he decided to take up show jumping seriously himself and, within a few weeks of the Victory Championship, had bought a horse in Leicestershire which, coming from that county, he christened Foxhunter. His great energy, ability and wealth were all put at the disposal of Colonel Mike Ansell and he was to play a major part in the revival of show jumping.

A party of Pony Club children came up to the White City that first Saturday in September 1945 in a coach party from the Cotswolds. Amongst them was the youthful Pat Smythe, who was so inspired that, as she tells in her famous first book *Jump for Joy,* she was determined to emulate the feats of those riders she had watched with such admiration and envy; two years later, when still in her teens, she was herself competing in the International Horse Show at the White City on her little mare, Finality. Not only was she competing but she was, in fact, defeating the best riders in Europe and before the end of the year she was herself to represent Britain in international show jumping.

Finally, it might not be inappropriate to mention that I myself was present in the audience that afternoon and very impressed, indeed excited, by it I was. A few nights later I was having dinner at the Cavalry Club with Mike Ansell – a very old friend of my family – and he asked me for my impressions. They were enthusiastic, as indeed had been everyone's. 'But surely,' he said, 'you must have some criticism; there must have been something that you thought could be done better?'

Because, for the first time, a show had been presented with the care and attention to detail of a theatrical production, it was not easy to find anything to criticise, but I did recall something that had caused a certain amount of inconvenience. I explained this to him. When a horse came in, the number of it and its name, and the name of the rider, was announced, but the result was not given immediately; it might be three or four horses later that the score of the original horse was announced and then, as only the number and not the name was given, it was easy to have forgotten which horse was having his score announced. By the time one had scanned through one's programme to find the relevant number one had either forgotten what the score was or had missed half the round of the horse then jumping. This seemed to me to be clumsy and inefficient, and I suggested that it could, perhaps, be improved.

Readers who know Colonel Mike Ansell as well as I, and all those who have worked with him for over a quarter of a century, will already have guessed his reply.

'Well, you can bloody well do it yourself!'

And so, when the International Horse Show was revived

at the White City in 1947, I was entrusted with the task of interpreting to a lay public what was then an almost completely unknown sport; so that great moment in show jumping in 1945 was also a great moment for me : though whether it made a great moment for the British public – especially the viewing public – is another matter !

Chapter XIV: *Olympia in the Old Days*

When the International Horse Show was first held at Olympia – it was actually started in 1907 – jumping played a very minor part. The carriage and the carriage horse were fast disappearing from the town streets and country roads as more and more people became infatuated with the recently-invented motor car. Not surprisingly, when the promotors of a show wanted to draw the attention of the public to the beauty, the elegance and the practicability of the horse-drawn vehicle and horses and ponies, it was to the United States that they turned for money, for even in those far-off days the Americans were proud of the standard of their harness horses and their equipages.

Under the presidency of the great Yellow Earl, Lord Lonsdale, the greatest name in sport at that time, this fabulous show was launched, but jumping seemed almost out of place in the extraordinary Olympia that was created for the show before the First World War. The decor alone made Cecil B. de Mille look almost a pauper. Vast, lantern-shaped chandeliers were suspended from the roof, while the floor and the tiers of seats were a sea of gilt and flowers–great banks of hydrangeas and huge baskets of carnations surrounding the whole arena; one side, where the boxes were placed, being covered with gilt chairs.

In the early days – and show jumping had only come to Britain at the beginning of the century – civilian riders were virtually unknown; show jumping was very much a sport for the military and, although in the 'twenties and 'thirties after the founding of the British Show Jumping Association, there were a number of civilian names in the show jumping

which were to become famous far beyond the horse world –
names such as Tommy Glencross, the Taylor brothers, the
Foster brothers (after one of whom the famous Wembley
Puissance is named), the Miss Bullows – yes, right up to the
Second World War, the show jumping was dominated by
cavalry officers, their regiments and, in the international
field, military teams. It is a fact that the first civilian rider
ever to win an international competition in show jumping
was Colonel Harry Llewellyn on Kilgeddin, in Rome in 1947.

Looking back, then, the names that dominated the show
jumping scene in those days were names of serving officers
from all countries; names perhaps which do not mean very
much today and yet by those who went to Olympia in those
early years after the First World War believed to be the
finest horsemen in the world – and who is to say that they
were not? For older readers, names such as Taffy Walwyn,
Talbot-Ponsonby, Dick Friedberger, Dolly de Fonblanque,
Howard Vyse, C. H. M. Brunker will awaken echoes. There
were also the great Irish riders – Dan Corrie, Jack Lewis,
O'Dwyer. From Belgium there was Van der Meersch; from
Italy Allesandro Bettoni; from France the immaculate,
monocled Bizard. These were great names in those days,
and their horses were no less famous – Red Hugh, Tramore
Bay, Limerick Lace – three of the greatest Irish horses that
ever jumped internationally; Goblet, Kineton, Blue Dun –
these were great British horses : and there were many others
which one felt one was privileged to see if they were jumping when one went to the International.

Today the Prince of Wales Cup – the team event – is not
usually considered the most important or, indeed, the most
exciting class at the Royal International Horse Show, though,
on the continent, the Nations' Cup still holds pride of place
at many shows, but at Olympia in the old days it was the
King George V Gold Cup, the great individual championship, and the Prince of Wales Cup that were the highlights
of the show; the performances that were called the Gala

Performances (it is interesting now to recall that they were both afternoon performances, for in those days before television and when there was still very much an elite society, the Wednesday afternoon at Olympia was as much a social occasion as Gold Cup day at Ascot or the Men's Finals at Wimbledon).

The event which I am going to describe may not historically be one of the great moments in show jumping yet surely it was a memorable occasion, and it was to make a lasting impression on a young schoolboy who had managed with great difficulty to get permission to attend the show (the headmaster finally relented when he was told by my housemaster that I had hunting pictures on my braces!). For one attending the International Horse Show at Olympia for the first time, the sight as one entered that great stadium was unforgettable, as was the atmosphere. The great banks of hydrangeas at each end of the arena; the smartly liveried attendants; great yellow drays – horse-drawn – to carry in fences; a huge backcloth at one end representing Lowther Castle; the flower-bedecked boxes with their gilt chairs; rows of vast, pink-shaded lamps hanging from the roof – these had replaced the pre-war lanterns. There were, too, the ring guard blowing his lengthy horn; the fine, expensive-looking rosettes; the music from the band, and always in the centre of the arena the legendary Lord Lonsdale himself, top hat, frock coat, Churchillian cigar and his famous sideboards. It was all unbelievably elegant, and what dignity the show then had.

Naturally the Prince of Wales Cup dominated that afternoon. It was all the more exciting, I remember, because for five years Britain had not been in the picture at all. It was the Irish, with their beautiful big, quality horses, that dominated the jumping scene, while already the riders from Italy and France were a threat, even in the highest grade of show jumping.

In those days the scoring was slightly different in that it

was still 4 faults for a knock-down with the forelegs and only 2 faults for a knock-down with the hind legs, but it was simple enough to score and I can see now the increasingly crumpled piece of paper in my programme, on which I wrote down the score for each of the four riders in each team – as today, they all jumped twice.

There was a long interval which could almost be likened to between races in the Royal Enclosure at Ascot or the interval at the Eton and Harrow Match at Lords in the old days, when around the stadium there was a perambulation of all the beauty and elegance that London could muster: how proud one felt to be a part of it, but how one longed to get back to the jumping. It was obvious that the result was going to be extremely close. Britain had jumped far better than had been anticipated, and it really did seem that if they could hold their own in the second round they might just pull it off.

Round by round the tension mounted. For a small boy at his first big show it was almost overwhelming, particularly as in those days patriotism (especially with the young) was far more fashionable than it is today.

I can remember now working out how much longer the competition would last; wondering if I could possibly stand this suspense until the end. I prayed to myself that our riders would not let us down. I can feel, as I write, the skin drawn taut across my cheeks and the breathless sensation which was heightened rather than relieved when Britain had a good round. Most of all I remember working out again and again the relevant scores, because then as now in the Nations' Cup the best three of the team of four counted. 'If the next Irish horse gets 8 faults; then if Kineton goes clear, we could still win' – 'If Limerick Lace goes clear for Ireland, then Goblet will have to have a clear round for Britain' – 'If Blue Dun has another fence down, then surely – why can't Tramore Bay hit a fence for once?'

This sensation of gnawing anxiety about a sport of which

I really knew very little was something quite new to me; I just had not realised that I could feel so excited. Once, a year or two earlier, I had seen a Cup replay with an hysterical audience of about forty thousand; I had once seen an exciting finish in the Boat Race; I had been on the rails fifty yards from the post when Windsor Lad won the Derby; I had thrilled with pride when Northamptonshire – my home county but, when I was at school, always bottom of the table – went very near to beating Australia at cricket; I had seen Obolensky's fantastic try at the end of a seventy-five yard run in the Varsity rugger match and seen Robson's famous dropped goal in the last minutes for Oxford at Twickenham – yet I had never felt anything quite like this.

It may have been because it was to do with horses, which was very much the background of our home and family life; it may have been because I was paying my first visit to this fantastic show at Olympia; it may have been that, as a boy in the 'twenties, one was more affected by patriotic sentiments than boys are today – I don't know. What I *do* know is that, when Goblet came in for the last round for Britain, I just did not know how I was going to contain myself.

Goblet was ridden by Colonel Joe Dudgeon, jumping at that time for the British team, being in the Scots Greys, though later he became even more famous as an Irish rider setting up after the Second World War his famous riding school just outside Dublin. Goblet had to do a clear round for Britain to win. I cannot recall now anything about that round, or even the fences, except that they looked very different and old-fashioned in that long, narrow arena at Olympia, but I do know that Joe Dudgeon and Goblet achieved that clear round and so gave victory to Britain.

I will not deny that, when the British team lined up in the centre of the arena and the band played 'God Save the King', there was a great lump in my throat and my eyes were smarting – not a very edifying state of affairs for a teenage schoolboy, but I was not the only one; indeed, I am prepared to swear that there were many damp eyes and throats so constricted that people found it impossible to speak.

I personally, and perhaps many others in that stadium which held only eight thousand, had had their first experience of the thrill of top-class show jumping. It is for this reason that I feel justified in including it as a great moment, for indeed, is there a greater moment in show jumping for any individual than the first time he feels really involved, has his emotions really stretched and finds himself caring desperately about the result.

That Prince of Wales Cup in the late 'twenties – or was it the very early 'thirties? – may not have been historical or of particular importance as far as the whole story of show jumping is concerned but, for one member of the audience, it was to have tremendous importance and so it was, for that member of the audience at any rate, one of show jumping's great moments.

For the record, it may be worth mentioning a few of the great names in that between-the-wars period in addition to those mentioned earlier in the chapter. Amongst the military riders there were: General Geoffrey Brooke, Major Lawrence, Colonel Gibbon, Colonel Malise Graham, Colonel V. D. S. Williams, Colonel 'Bebe' Cameron, Colonel Nat Kindersley, Captain Mike Ansell. The civilian riders included Frank Allison, Henry Buckland, Phil Blackmore, Syd Woodhall, Tommy Makin, Sam Marsh and Lady Wright – one of the Miss Bullows sisters. They were to be joined a little later by such as Ted Williams, 'Curly' Beard, Andrew Massarella. Some of the more famous horses were: Swank, Toby, Desire, Bronco, Chelsea, Combined Training, Stuck Again, Silver Mint.

These names may not mean very much to those who were brought up on Harvey Smiths and David Broomes, Marion Moulds and Ann Moores, on Mattie Browns and Psalms and Pennwood Forge Mills, but they were part of the history of show jumping in Britain and indeed, a very vital part.

Chapter XV: *Olympia Again*

Considerable interest was shown, in the week before Christmas 1972, in the mounting of a new show at Olympia. For so long between 1907 and the Second World War, Olympia had been the venue for some of the greatest show jumping in the world; indeed, the name was synonymous with an international horse show of the very highest standard. It is probably true to say that the shows at Olympia before the First World War and in the 'twenties and 'thirties set a standard for international shows the world over.

Since 1939 there had been no horse show at Olympia, and therefore no show jumping. Rather, Olympia had become famous for Bertram Mills's great Christmas circus. It was a clever idea, therefore, of Messrs Dunhills, to propose a show which was in effect a mixture of show jumping and circus. The decision to hold it the week before Christmas was, perhaps, fortuitous, as no other week seemed available. Nevertheless, this particular time in the calendar did give an opportunity for the organisers to mingle circus events of an equestrian nature with major show jumping events.

Undoubtedly the engagement of the famous Liberty horses that used to be presented by the Schumann family, and now presented by Mary Chipperfield – another famous circus name – set the seal on the circus spirit, but there were other displays which gave great pleasure, especially to the large numbers of children who came to the show. There was a Pony Club display of Snow White and the Seven Dwarfs; there was a comic horse-drawn fire engine; there was a quadrille performed by a riding club, all six of its members being dressed as clowns. These divertissements were understandably highly popular. Most popular of all, perhaps, was the finale 'A Christmas Card comes to Life'. In this charming display four horse-drawn vehicles, each accompanied by two riders – one astride and one side-saddle – the personnel all wearing Dickensian costume – performed a delightful quadrille to suitable and very well-known Christmas music, while brief extracts were read from Dickens's most famous Christmas passages in *The Pickwick Papers* – Christmas at Dingley Dell. At the end, in a sleigh drawn by four small ponies, Father Christmas himself came in and, on reaching the centre, snow began to fall from the roof, rather like poppies fall from the roof of the Albert Hall at the Festival of Remembrance. The effect, in the lighting, and in the unique atmosphere of Olympia, was charming – particularly on the final night when the Royal Mail coach galloped into the arena, drawn by four spanking bays, the coach itself already so decorated that it gave the impression of having been driven through the snow, the passengers being many of the more famous show jumpers taking part – all, of course, in Dickensian costume. With the snow falling from the roof, also falling on the coach, a choir of red-cassocked choristers joined the centre-piece to lead the vast audience in popular carols.

This was something that even Olympia had never seen before, but it was, of course, a show jumping event that Dunhills were putting on. Thanks to the generous prize money, leading riders from all over Europe were attracted to the show; but, as was the case at the Horse of the Year Show and the Courvoisier Championships at Wembley, it was the German riders who dominated the main events. This was hardly surprising in view of the fact that Alwin Schockemöhle with his great horse, The Robber, and his brother Paul, were leading a contingent of German riders all of whom were well known internationally, two of whom had Olympic status: the other was Hartwig Steenken with the outstanding mare Simona, which although no longer young, is still reckoned one of the greatest horses jumping in

Europe – certainly she was at her very best at Olympia in an arena which was slightly larger than the arena at Wembley and which, after the first day, provided first class going.

The show was, in fact, extremely popular with the riders from the very start. This was partially due to the fact that the stables, the practice ring and the main arena were all under one roof, which made it very convenient for the competitors. It was partially due, too, to the relaxed atmosphere made possible by a show which, simple in its intentions, was not all the time pressing against the clock to try and fit in a full and varied programme for the satisfaction of all sections of the public. The terms of reference here were much more basic; two major jumping competitions, one at each end of the performance, and in between a series of turns designed to entertain at quite a humble level, with an interval of at least twenty minutes enabling people to wander at leisure amongst the stands, or patronise the bars. In fact, this sort of tempo is very much more the tempo of the continental show; in Britain we have always prided outselves on the slickness of presentation so that, in one performance, a great variety of equestrianism can be presented with the programme never falling behind the clock. At Olympia there was no attempt to emulate this presentation and so, not surprisingly perhaps, there was from one or two sources a criticism of the somewhat easy-going presentation. It may be, however, that this was – on this particular occasion – more to the liking of the spectators, for it must be remembered that running a show immediately before Christmas inevitably means that a very large proportion of the audience is made up of children.

As already stated, the German team dominated the jumping competitions despite the absence of World Champion and four-time Olympic gold medallist Hans Winkler, who, surprisingly, and to the great disappointment of the organisers – and indeed, many others – failed to turn up. It may be that Winkler had a good reason for not turning up, despite the fact that, twenty-four hours before the show started, he was on the telephone to the B.S.J.A. and did not mention that he was not coming. One wonders sometimes whether great personalities in the entertainment world – and show jumping is now part of the entertainment world – realise how great is the disappointment that they cause when they fail to turn up having been announced. It is a pity when people whose names are famous in any sphere treat the world that has made them famous in a cavalier fashion; more than that, they might even be making the show liable to litigation, for to advertise the presence of a famous name who then does not turn up could well make a show liable to a summons under the Trade Descriptions Act. Unfortunately, in all show business, there seems to be an increasing tendency for stars to fail to turn up although their presence has been widely announced.

The very first competition on the opening day of the show was won by Alwin Schockemöhle, with the Frenchman Jean Chabrol second. David Broome was the only British rider to be seriously knocking at the door – a situation which continued all the week. The first major event was won by Hartwig Steenken with Simona; France again was second with Jean-Michel Gaud. On Wednesday the major events were both won by Alwin Schockemöhle with Weier and The Robber, Broome being runner-up again in the first event while Paddy McMahon on Pennwood Forge Mill was runner-up in the second, giving the audience hope, therefore, that he might be preparing to pull off another coup such as he did on the last night of the Horse of the Year Show.

It was, however, on the Thursday evening that we had the first real taste of greatness in a major international competition. This was the puissance. With so strong a German contingent there was a formidable-looking field and certainly the first round gave the impression that this was going to be a hotly disputed competition, with the 7 ft. 3 in.

that Ray Howe jumped at Wembley on Kalkallo Prince, being exceeded. However, it was not to work out this way for, in the fourth round when there were still seven horses left in, the decision was made to increase the height of the final wall to 7 ft. 1 in. This was a rise of 6 in.

There is always a problem in the puissance; the bricks are either three inches or six inches; only four jump-offs are allowed, so if the course builder increases the height of a fence in units which are too small, then the likelihood is that one will finish with a large number of horses equal first, having jumped a not particularly high fence. The decision was made, therefore, to go up to 7 ft. 1 in. Obviously there were certain people who felt that this was too steep a rise, and indeed for a long time it looked as if they were right and there was going to be a disappointing result, with certainly four and probably five equal firsts.

In fact, many of the most famous horses failed to clear the wall at 7 ft. 1 in.; these included Raymond Howe on Kalkallo Prince, who had jumped that dramatic 7 ft. 3 in. at Wembley (but who had failed to beat the British high jump record, 7 ft. 6½ in., held since 1936 by Donald Beard on Swank, in a special event put on at Olympia on the Wednesday evening); Captain Kiely on that really good Irish horse Inis Cara; Ted Edgar, who had been in great form all the week and constantly knocking at the door, riding Everest Snaffles; and Paddy McMahon on Pennwood Forge Mill, who only just failed to clear the 7 ft. 3 in. wall at Wembley. They all failed now at 7 ft. 1 in. and all made the wall look really difficult.

There was only one other rider to come. This was that great artist from Brazil, now living in Europe – Nelson Pessoa. In fact his form during 1972 had been consistently disappointing; his performance in the Olympic Games in Munich had been almost a disaster, though he himself attributed this to the fact that, as he was jumping as an individual and not as a member of a team, it was impossible to give his horse sufficient work once he had got it to Munich. Whatever the reason his horse in Munich was extremely disappointing.

It is always exciting when a rider with a great reputation but a current loss of form – or perhaps has gone over the top altogether – suddenly makes a dramatic come-back. It happened the first year that the Royal International went to Wembley, when Alan Oliver appeared on Sweep, which he had taken over for Mr Cawthraw after the tragic death of Chris Jackson who up to then had ridden him. Alan's two victories at Wembley, after a long period in the wilderness, were amongst the most popular victories that I ever remember in show jumping. So it was that many were hoping that the almost legendary Nelson Pessoa, who for so long, by so many, had been considered one of the greatest riders in the world, could at last stage a come-back.

He did in no uncertain manner. Riding Odeon, he met the big parallels exactly right and made them look very easy. He then turned and faced the big, red wall. He rode down to it on this light-framed, wiry little horse a good deal faster than most of his rivals had. He met it absolutely perfectly and, standing well back, it was quite obvious that he had a real chance of clearing it. In fact, he did hit the coping stone at the top of the wall, slightly dislodging it, but fortunately it stayed put and Odeon landed neatly to the enormous cheer from the great and sympathetic crowd.

This was a real and rewarding come-back for this charming and talented horseman, who has brought over so many potential young jumpers from South America, schooled them on and sold them to become leading jumpers for leading riders in Europe.

Just to show that his victory was by no means a flash in the pan, on the following day – the last day of the show – Pessoa won another major event on Odeon, but the final victory went almost inevitably one felt to Germany, and once again it was Hartwig Steenken on Simona – the combination that had won the first major event of the show.

But Steenken did not have it all his own way. There is little doubt that David Broome could very easily have won the Victor Ludorum on that last night at Olympia. He turned into the wall, the last fence, impossibly tight and, as it turned out, unnecessarily tight, for he had the best part of two seconds in hand; but Ballywillwill just could not get round the corner, and so ran into the wing at the side of the wall.

The biggest surprise, however, was the performance of young Malcolm Bowey from Durham; a twenty-year-old student of John Lanni, who, of course, is one of the great Massarella clan – riding a little-known horse called Partington. He really did give Steenken the fright of his life as his horse was jumping so well that, having had a double clear in this two-round finale, it was quite obvious that Simona, coming after Partington, would have to take something of a risk and chance a fence down. However, Partington was not quite fast enough and had to be content with second place.

But it is this sort of thing that is the very stuff of show jumping : the sudden appearance on the scene of someone totally unknown challenging the might of the world. It happened some twenty-five years earlier when Pat Smythe and Finality suddenly appeared at the White City in the Royal International Horse Show, and won major competitions in the very teeth of the strongest possible international opposition. It happened when Harvey Smith first appeared on Farmer's Boy; when David Broome first appeared on Wildfire. It will go on happening, and it is because new names, unknown to the general public, will keep suddenly appearing to challenge the great names which are world famous, that show jumping will remain popular. There is no certainty about show jumping – even Foxhunter failed at Helsinki. Even Askan, the German horse which had cost nearly £60,000, failed at Munich. Even Mancinelli, having won the individual gold medal in the 1972 Olympics, flopped completely in the team event on his gold medal horse.

In other words, the horse is not a machine and the rider is only human; so there will always be the dramas of the unexpected, the challenge of the Goliaths by the unheard-of Davids, and the failures and the come-backs, as demonstrated by Pessoa at Olympia in December 1972.

Jump Off

Some reader may ask how on earth can that marvellous duel for the King George V Gold Cup in 1954, when Alan Oliver and Red Admiral battled it out with Fritz Theidemann on Meteor round after round, be omitted? Or surely, another reader will say, the marvellous occasion when Carlos Figuroa won the King George V in 1952 on Gracieux, should have been included. The highly emotional way he flung his arm round his horse's neck and kissed it is one of the highlights of show jumping.

Then what about Seamus Hayes glorious victory in the Hickstead Derby on Goodbye? Or the other great Irish victory in Rome, in 1962, when dramatically Capt. Billy Ringrose achieved the only clear round in the Grand Prix? Dramatic in more sense than one, incidentally, as thanks to there being only one clear round, the whole competition was practically over before the arrival of the Queen, who was paying a state visit to Italy: it would have been finished had it not been for a massive 'go-slow' in the running of the competition!

There was the Olgiata at the Rome Show, too, in 1969 when Anneli Drummond-Hay won it so sensationally with the only clear round on the little Xanthos, an ex-hunt servant's horse. What a spectacle this mixture of show jumping and cross country provided. And how dramatic it was for the B.B.C. when, thanks to a strike, there would have been no television had not the B.B.C. flown in a camera crew which had to pretend to be private enthusiasts for fear of being 'blacked'.

Anneli, in fact, was involved in what was for me an even

greater moment of show jumping later the same year. I had been invited as Honorary Director of the National Equestrian Centre, to attend the opening of a huge new school, the centre of a property complex sixty miles outside Los Angeles. In addition to the National Equestrian Centre Manager, Charles Stratton, and Chief Instructor, Bill Froud, I had been invited to take two leading riders. Anneli Drummond-Hay and Alan Oliver were the two who came.

An international event was arranged with riders from America, Canada, Mexico and Britain. The visitors were provided with horses. Anneli was offered a five-year-old grey of, approximately, Foxhunter Competition (novice) standard. By the end of the week she had got this novice going so well that it qualified for the Victor Ludorum. Finally there was a jump-off against the clock between Anneli and Barbara Simpson of Canada, one of the leading lady riders in the world, on an international horse.

Barbara went first and going clear, clocked a really fast time. Then Anneli set her little grey alight, and in one of the most brilliant, inspired bits of riding that I have ever seen in my life she beat Barbara by half a second.

This, for my memory, was show jumping at its greatest and compensated a little for my being electrocuted by a faulty microphone at the opening session! made even more unreal, incidentally, when by some million to one chance instead of the Chief Instructor's voice coming out of the radio mike he was using, a talk that I had recorded on the B.B.C.'s World Service *three years earlier* suddenly boomed forth – presumably being broadcast somewhere on the same wavelength!

But, of course, there are so many occasions, so many incidents: dramatic, exciting, odd, farcical even; but always interesting. One could, perhaps, write an entirely different book. But the foregoing chapters, for what they are worth, include moments in show jumping history which I believe to be the most worthy recording for posterity. They span fifty years : they spell success and sorrow, triumph and disaster.

And they all inevitably reflect a personal viewpoint, for having been present at each occasion included I have only been able to describe them as I experienced them.

I can only hope that I have been able to impart a little of the excitement and pleasure that they have brought to me.

INDEX